CW00393680

PRAISE FC
PRAYER, MEDICINE, /

"Human need for and experience of healing reach back to the earliest dawn of creation and will remain as long as mankind exists on the earth. Healing—natural and supernatural—is rooted in God, who said, 'I am the LORD who heals you.' (Exod 15:26). Jesus was a healer, and He commissioned all His followers to heal the sick.

"In *Prayer, Medicine, and Healing*, Thomson Mathew gives compelling biblical, historical, existential, and personal evidence for the credibility of healing. A rich blend of scholarly rigor, theological fidelity, and pastoral sensitivity, the book presents a balanced view of various models of healing and personalities in the healing movement. Mathew irreversibly believes that 'God responds to the prayer of faith for healing and wholeness offered in the name of Jesus.' Everyone should, therefore, pray for the sick with an expectant faith.

"As the title of the book betrays, Mathew believes God uses prayer and medicine to heal. Neither method should be rejected. While emphasizing the importance of faith for healing, he cautions that faith does not guarantee a positive outcome. God's sovereignty is an essential part of a biblical theology of healing. Mathew hopes that 'all followers of Jesus . . . will see . . . their responsibility to pray for the sick by faith.'"

—**Trevor Grizzle**, PhD, professor of New Testament, Graduate School of Theology and Ministry, Oral Roberts University

"The lack of an accurate biblical understanding of health and healing is, unfortunately, commonplace in the body of Christ today. Even among followers of Jesus who work in health care, this is true. My friend Dr. Thomson Mathew has studied and researched and investigated very thoroughly this important area, and in this book provides a thoughtful and comprehensive treatise for us all. Rather than basing his conclusions on his personal experience or intellectual musings, he has looked deeply into the Scriptures (both Old and New Testaments), the life of Jesus Christ, the early church, and faithful men and women who were followers of Jesus to provide an outstanding resource for those of us who desire to know the truth.

"As a physician, I want to follow in the steps of Jesus. It is recorded that 'He went around doing good and healing all that were afflicted by the devil, because God was with Him!' (Acts 10:38, paraphrased). I remind my patients regularly that I cannot heal them, but Jesus can! This book will encourage us to pray in faith for the sick, to care deeply and compassionately for those who are suffering, and to demonstrate the love of God to those in desperate need."

—**Mitch Duininck**, MD, FAAFP, president and CEO, In His Image (IHI), IHI International, and Good Samaritan Health Services, Tulsa, Oklahoma; director, IHI Family Medicine Residency Program; and president, Oklahoma Academy of Family Physicians

"One of the most important elements of true Christianity is the fact that God is alive and active. The miracles of healing have abounded in the history of the church. Thomson K. Mathew, in his book *Prayer, Medicine, and Healing,* argues convincingly that despite some efforts of modern skeptics who would reduce the reality of Christian faith to an entirely spiritual realm, there is actually a good cause for embracing both natural and supernatural dimensions of our salvation, manifested also in physical cure. The excellent contribution is the presence of a very balanced theological view harmonizing biblical certainty of healing and God's sovereignty where there is sufficient room for both medicine and prayer. I recommend the material to everyone who is eager to pursue the full gospel and had previous doubts about how medical science and divine healing go well together."

—**Pavel Hoffman**, BA, MA, MDiv, PhD (candidate), Bible translator and theologian at Scandinavian School of Theology, Uppsala, Sweden

"With decades of experience as chaplain, pastor, and dean, Dr. Mathew presents a unique perspective in the area of health and healing. He not only teaches theology but also imparts from the depth of his personal life and ministry. As a graduate of Oral Roberts University, I was greatly inspired by Dr. Mathew's stories of faith and healing.

"This book addresses an essential topic for the body of Christ today. It will deepen your theological understanding and also challenge you to pray boldly for the sick. I highly recommend this book to pastors, leaders, Bible school students, and anyone who wants to experience God's healing power in life and ministry."

—**Rev. Charleston Lim,** executive leadership team, Heart of God Church, Singapore

"I met Dr. Thomson Mathew while I was a young seminary student exploring God's call on my life. Growing up during the charismatic movement of the 1980s and 1990s, I witnessed God's healing power but was ill-equipped to articulate a clear and mature theology of pastoral care and healing.

"Dr. Mathew led me on a journey through his classes, his life, and his ministry toward a deeper and richer understanding of God's healing power. He exemplified how a pastor can embrace healing from a biblical, theological, historical, and experiential way.

"The content of this book is not written by someone who has only researched a topic. The content comes from Dr. Mathew's lifetime of work as a true practitioner, a pastor, a chaplain, and an educator.

"His heart of genuine care for people is evident in his writing. Whether you are a medical professional, a minister, or someone who is searching to understand God's healing power, the content in this text will inspire you to see God as your healer. We are fearfully and wonderfully made, body, mind, and spirit, and God brings wholeness to every area of brokenness. The prayer of faith for healing is powerful and is needed more today than ever."

—**Dr. Barry Simon,** executive pastor/ministries director, The Assembly at Broken Arrow, Broken Arrow, Oklahoma

"Dr. Thomson Mathew provides a comprehensive look at how prayer, medicine, and divine healing work hand in hand to provide individual wholeness. Having been a pastor, chaplain, and educator, he draws from his vast experience to provide the reader with a biblically based, historically informed, and theologically sound foundation for the real-world, real-time practice of divine healing. Mathew demonstrates that it is more than a forgotten historical practice, as cessation theology would like us to believe. He strikes a key balance between the biblical certainty of healing and the sovereignty of God when divine healing does not occur immediately. He gives place to both supernatural healing through the "Great Physician" and natural healing through the hands of a human caregiver. Having been a student and colleague under his tutelage, I can testify that his belief in healing prayer is a regular life practice and not just a theory that is never tested. He truly believes that all Christians have a responsibility to pray in faith for the sick."

—**Dr. Tim Ekblad,** assistant professor of practical theology and director of the Modular and Distance Education Program, College of Theology and Ministry, Oral Roberts University

"The subject of healing has been taboo in many denominations. Even within Pentecostal and charismatic churches, the practice of healing and the expectation of one receiving healing have become scarce. That is why I am so excited about Dr. Thomson K. Mathew's book *Prayer, Medicine, and Healing.* With sound theology, a look at the church's historical and practical stance on the subject, and a scholarly logic, Mathew calls for all Christians to begin to pray for the sick. Mathew's work with both a healing evangelist (where miracles took place) and a team of chaplains at a hospital (where surgeries and medication were given) gives him a unique perspective on the subject that he tackles in this book. There is little doubt that the reader will capture (or recapture) a reasonable faith and expectation of God's healing power. This book is a tool to empower people to pray for sick, whether at the altar or on the surgical table, and expect God to heal."

—**Rev. Michael McAfee,** evangelist, Nashville, Tennessee

"No one is better equipped to address the issue of prayer, medicine, and healing than Dr. Thomson K. Mathew. Raised in India, where his grandparents and his parents trained him in the foundation of biblical principles, he developed his gifted intellect while attending Yale University Divinity School. God used his talents as a pastor, chaplain, professor of pastoral care, and ultimately as the dean of the College of Theology and Ministry at Oral Roberts University. It was through these phases that Dr. Mathew worked alongside Oral Roberts to help refine the concept of merging prayer and medicine. He has witnessed numerous healings by prayer as well as medicine and is always comfortable to offer prayer for healing.

"Dr. Mathew has done an excellent review of the history of healing ministry and the work of hospitals. He also has shared renowned Christian leaders he has personally known who have demonstrated the effectiveness of praying for the sick. The conclusion of the book provides documentation that healing is for today, and as followers of Jesus, we should be willing to pray for healing of the sick.

"I have known Dr. Mathew since 1982. He has been a bright light to all who met him as he shared the reality of merging healing prayer and medicine to bring wholeness to people. Dr. Mathew demonstrated his faith in God and His healing power daily, both at City of Faith Medical Center and Oral Roberts University, where I interacted with him. He is truly a man of God and a role model for all."

—**Dr. Glenda Payas,** DMD, former member of the Board of Regents and the Board of Trustees, Oral Roberts University

"The relationship between faith healing and traditional medicine has been contentious over the years. The teaching and practice of divine healing have been consistently scrutinized, challenged, and debated, particularly of late within the context of the COVID-19 pandemic.

"In this book, Dr. Thomson K. Mathew masterfully presents a balanced view between faith healing and medicine, based on biblical, historical, and doctrinal aspects. His unique perspective encourages readers to form a healthy personal understanding of these complex issues.

"I have found the book to be intellectually stimulating, theologically rooted, and biblically sound and believe that Dr. Mathew's profound expertise and insights reflected in every page will create a ripple effect and benefit both the theologically trained as well as laypeople in Christendom today.

"I congratulate Dr. Thomson K. Mathew for his seminal contribution to the global church through this book and pray that it encourages and blesses the universal body of Christ."

—**Rev. Dr. Abraham Mathew,** principal,
New Life College, Bangalore, India

"In his latest book, *Prayer, Medicine, and Healing,* Dr. Thomson K. Mathew takes us on a journey through Scripture and church history to discover God's healing power throughout the centuries. He clearly displays that at no time in history has God taken a break from healing the sick, whether through natural or supernatural means. Combining scholarly insight, pastoral sensitivity, and firsthand experiences of a living God, he shows us a path forward to minister healing to others."

"The apostle Paul once wrote, 'For the kingdom of God is not a matter of talk but of power.' (1 Cor 4:20 NIV). In our day, Dr. Mathew has lived out this biblical truth in his own life and ministry and has therefore been able to teach it to many all over the world. I encourage you to go through this book with an open heart and an open mind. I have no doubt that you will receive a fresh revelation of Christ the healer."

—**Rev. Sam Barsoum,** director, Bible
Institute, Oral Roberts University

"Prayer, medicine, and healing are important concepts of great interest to Christians everywhere. Unfortunately, it is difficult to find biblically sound, scholarly, and easily readable books on these subjects from a whole-person perspective. Dr. Thomson K. Mathew has managed to address this need in an outstanding way. His hard work has produced a guidebook providing an evangelical understanding of healing and the importance of prayer and an invitation to experience biblical healing. I sincerely hope this book will be read by followers of Jesus in all walks of life.

"Having seen a translation of his book *Spirit-Led Ministry in the 21st Century* causing a great sensation in the Korean church, it has been my privilege to translate his recent volume titled *Spiritual Identity and Spirit-Empowered Life* into the Korean language. I hope that *Prayer, Medicine, and Healing* will also have a great influence on the English-speaking readers as well as Korean Christians."

—**Joseph Jeon,** DMin, EdD, PhD, professor, Sungkyul University; chaplain major (retd.), Republic of Korea Military; and former president, Academic Association of Evangelical Practical Theology, Korea

PRAYER, MEDICINE & HEALING

PRAYER, MEDICINE & HEALING

Why Ministers, Medical Professionals, and All Followers of Jesus Should Pray for the Sick

THOMSON K. MATHEW

To two family members:

the late Rev. K. C. John (Pathichira Yohannachan),
a pastor who prayed for the sick,
and
Dr. Fiju V. Koshy, a physician who cares about his patients

CONTENTS

FOREWORD

Out of his background in pastoral care, theology, and education, Dr. Thomson K. Mathew has created another book, this one on healing, both natural and divine. In this volume, he sends forth a needed call to everyone concerned to emphasize and reemphasize the subject of healing in today's church. He also issues a warning that the subject of healing is too often neglected.

How can this work be adequately described? Is it a guide-book? Is it a manual of training? A treatise? A theological position paper? A survey of the healing ministry? A plea for practice? My answer is yes, yes to all of these!

Dr. Mathew points out that Jesus came "preaching, teaching, and healing." He indicates that ministry is not meant to be a single-task enterprise, so why do we often make it to mean that we can reduce healing while lifting preaching and teaching? Addressing this situation, he provides a balance to the subject by bringing together the streams of theology, history, Scripture, and practice. He also presents various opinions and positions on healing and reviews them carefully.

Mathew was privileged to have Oral Roberts, the forerunner of modern healing evangelism, as a mentor and ministry partner at the City of Faith Hospital, established on the campus of Oral Roberts University (ORU). As a chaplain and prayer partner, he went with Oral Roberts from room to room, praying for the sick and afflicted, and witnessed the power of the prayer of faith.

I recall a time when Roberts spoke to some faculty members and a group of doctoral students at ORU around a conference table. He began by holding out his hands toward us, saying something like, "These hands have been placed on, some say, a million people. The healing Savior touched many with His hands, including lepers and other untouchables." His point to the students was to "go and do likewise" (Luke 10:37).

As with Dr. Mathew's previous books, he presents a very practical approach to the subject. He is biblically sound, theologically supported, and historically accurate. His readers will be impacted and blessed.

—Kenneth Mayton, EdD, former professor and director of the Doctor of Ministry Program, Oral Roberts University

INTRODUCTION

I was raised in a pastor's home in Kerala, India. The oldest of six children, I grew up in very modest circumstances, hearing my father (Rev. K. Thomas Mathew) and grandfather (Rev. K. Mathew Thomas) preach about the Jesus who saves and heals. Their messages had a tremendous impact on my life. Having two grandmothers testifying of having received physical healing and one who survived several snakebites without any medical treatment and having a mother whose story paralleled that of the woman healed by touching the hem of Jesus' garment reinforced what my father and grandfather preached. In some remote places where my parents ministered, receiving immediate medical care was not an option. Even when it was available, medical care did not seem to be their preference in those days. On occasions when these loved ones were persuaded to seek medical care, I witnessed the positive outcomes of the work of doctors and nurses but did not know then how to connect these two streams of healing—divine healing and modern medicine.

My parents and grandparents were not known as healing ministers in India. They were pastors, shepherding individual congregations or overseeing an area of churches. This was not the case with the family of my wife, Molly. Her grandfather Pastor K. C. John (popularly known as Pathichira Yohannachan), whose name is in many primary sources of the history of the Pentecostal movement in India as an impactful person in the establishment of Pentecostalism in Kerala, was widely known as a healing minister. His autobiographical notes left behind and his biography written by Rev. B. Saji, a seminary professor in India, record numerous incidents of divine healing that took place under his ministry.[1] Molly's father (Pastor K. J. George), who pastored a congregation for forty years in Kayamkulam, Kerala, was also known as a person involved in healing ministry.

Sick people used to come to my wife's childhood residence and stay, often for days at a time. Her parents and other church members fasted and prayed for the sick, and many reported healings, some experiencing instant healing from physical ailments and several recovering from symptoms of mental illnesses. Once, Molly's mother was presumed dead (no doctor was there to formally pronounce it), and as church members rushed out to inform extended family members, her grandfather laid hands on her mother and prayed, and she woke up and spoke and lived to tell that story for another thirty years.

Molly's family was more resistant to medical treatment than my family. In fact, they personified divine healing to

---

[1] See B. Saji, *Oru Pravachakante Preshitha Yathra: A Prophet's Missionary Journey* (Kayamkulam, Kerala, India: Mizpah Publications, 2003).

such a degree that when Molly enrolled as a student in the nursing school at Mayo Hospital in Nagpur, several families left her home church, seeing her career plan as evidence of her parents' lack of faith in God the healer!

This book is not an anecdotal encyclopedia. I started this introduction with our family history to help you understand our background so you could fully appreciate the biblical, theological, historical, and practical reasons why I believe in natural and supernatural healing, or whole-person medicine and divine healing—both enhanced by prayer. Although you will see a synthesis of biblical, theological, and historical concepts in this book, this is more than a theological argument or a practical polemic; this book is a witness. It is the outcome of a journey of faith and learning that sent me from a preacher's home in India through Yale University Divinity School to Oral Roberts University.

The positive relationship between prayer and health has been studied and documented. Many of these studies are about prayer of all kinds, regardless of the religious assumptions and theologies undergirding the prayers. My interest is prayer for healing exclusively in the name of Jesus Christ. My interest is not in the science of the act of prayer, but in the theology and history of Christian prayer for healing. Likewise, Craig Keener and others have convincingly documented the authenticity of contemporary miracles.[2] I do not focus on miracles but presuppose the reality of authentic miracles and supernatural

---

[2] See Craig S. Keener, *Miracles Today: The Supernatural Work of God in the Modern World* (Grand Rapids: Baker Academic, 2021).

healings. This book is about prayer of faith as a Christian practice and ministry. I am interested in what the Bible has to say about it and how the church has (or has not) historically practiced it. Based on my own encounters with well-known Christian efforts to heal the sick, I hope to present a perspective that allows sick individuals to pray and seek divine healing without necessarily rejecting science-based medicine, especially whole-person medicine.

I am a graduate of Yale Divinity School (MDiv and STM) and Oral Roberts University Seminary (DMin). Obviously, these two schools represent vastly different theological perspectives and presuppositions. So, you will see the influence of both Henri Nouwen and Oral Roberts on my thinking in these pages. You will also encounter the simple review of biblical texts on healing as well as a theological and historical examination of divine healing.

After a year of clinical pastoral education (CPE) and five years of experience as the pastor of a New England church, I joined the chaplaincy staff of the former City of Faith Hospital in Tulsa, Oklahoma, which was founded by Oral Roberts as a part of the ORU medical school to merge medicine and prayer. (The story of the City of Faith is in this book.) Because Oral Roberts was a globally recognized healing evangelist, I had numerous opportunities to participate in his Pentecostal/charismatic healing ministry outside the hospital while, at the same time, working with highly competent medical doctors, nurses, and other professionals on the "healing teams" at the City of Faith. These practitioners were sincerely and intentionally endeavoring to mix the prayer of faith with competent, science-based medical practices, expecting better outcomes for the patients.

A host of clinically trained chaplains from different denominations who believed in the power of prayer and the current work of the Holy Spirit were also involved in the expensive City of Faith Medical and Research Center. This effort lasted only eight years due to financial challenges and other reasons, but this short-lived experiment, which had an undeniable impact on the medical world, gave everyone involved plenty of opportunities to "watch and pray" (Mark 13:33; 14:38) to see the implications of believing in both natural and supernatural healing in the twentieth century. Lessons learned from reflections on this experience are also in this book.

As home to the headquarters of several international ministries, including Rhema Bible College (Kenneth Hagin Sr.), T. L. Osborn Foundation, and Oral Roberts Ministries, among others, Tulsa, Oklahoma, has been considered the charismatic capital of the world. All sorts of revivalists, healing evangelists, and "miracle workers" came through Tulsa in the 1970s and '80s with their meetings and crusades, and I had many opportunities to observe the authentic and be stunned by the imitators. Some skeptics and cessationists (those who believe the gifts of the Holy Spirit, such as healings or miracles, ceased after the second century) use the work of the fake healers to discredit all healing ministries. Having witnessed the genuine work of God through some of His servants, I never could join them.

I have witnessed healing through medicine and prayer among my loved ones. I have a daughter who was healed of a serious case of childhood asthma through prayer after which she no longer required prescription medication. (I will not forget the moment in the intensive care unit of the City of Faith Hospital when this daughter asked me, "Daddy, am I dying?") I have a grandson (through the healed daughter) whom I saw for the first time as a swollen and intubated baby in a neonatal ICU in Oklahoma City, where he was struggling to breathe just hours after his birth in another, less-specialized hospital. He has been fully recovered through prayer and medical intervention, especially under the careful watch of his physician father. I also know several individuals who received healing simply through prayer, without any medical intervention.

The COVID-19 pandemic has changed the world in ways we do not fully understand yet. Over a million people died just in the United States. The arguments and counterarguments continue regarding the efficacy of vaccinations, preventive measures, herd immunity, and so on. This situation brought up many questions of faith and practice for believers and nonbelievers. I have heard sermons for and against immunization, isolation, and prayer for healing. One preacher asked, "Didn't COVID teach you to stop praying for healing and prepare for spiritual growth and heaven?" Some seem to say that since prayer did not stop the pandemic, we should not waste time praying for the sick. This is despite the "cloud of witnesses" (see Heb 12:1), including respiratory therapists and ICU workers, who survived, some having never been infected. I hope this book will show why all followers of Jesus should pray for the sick, not just for peace of mind, but for real healing.

Having never been in a hospital as a patient, I received a surprising diagnosis three years ago. While I was dealing with the illness, Judy Cope, my longtime administrative assistant at Oral Roberts University, sent me a list of one hundred scripture verses related to God's work of healing for my contemplation. I found the verses reassuring as my family, friends, and church prayed for me and I prayerfully cooperated with my physicians. My condition required major surgery by a skillful surgeon, but with only some over-the-counter Tylenol pills and no other medicines, I have fully recovered from my illness with no feared consequences. If you are in the midst of a medical challenge, I hope this book, like Mrs. Cope's gift of Bible verses, will encourage you to trust God and pray by faith no matter what your other treatment plans might be.

I am fully aware that personal experience is not the most reliable authority on matters of theology and doctrine. What does the Bible say about health and healing? What does the history of healing work—both divine healing ministry and medical treatment by physicians—teach us about health and healing? These important questions are central to this book.

Chapter 1 examines health and healing in the Hebrew Bible, focusing on Yahweh as the God who heals. Chapter 2 is a study of this topic in the New Testament, focusing on the life of Jesus and His disciples. I devote chapter 3 to Jesus' method of healing through word and touch. Chapter 4 presents a synthesis of the biblical perspective on healing. Chapter 5 is a history of healing from the early church fathers to the post-Reformation period, and chapter 6 details the development of a theology of divine healing in the intercontinental Holiness movement. This is followed by the history of healing in the Pentecostal/charismatic tradition in chapter 7.

Two twentieth-century healing ministers and their healing theologies are presented in this book, one representing an evangelistic model of healing ministry and the other a pastoral approach, both from a Pentecostal/charismatic perspective. Oral Roberts from the West is presented in chapter 8, followed by the story of the City of Faith Hospital in chapter 9. From the East, David Yonggi Cho, founding pastor of the largest Christian congregation in the world, in Seoul, Korea, is discussed in chapter 10. I hope that those who wish to minister to the sick as well as those who seek healing will gain important insights from these two ministers.

Chapter 11 is devoted to the history of hospitals and medical work as an extension of the compassionate work of Jesus and the unique concept of neighbor that He taught. Chapter 12 addresses the issues and challenges raised by the skeptics, cessationists, extremist prosperity preachers, and various contemporary Pentecostals who overreact to such prosperity preachers by not preaching about faith and healing at all. Finally, chapter 13 summarizes why I believe in divine healing and whole-person medicine and pray for the sick in an almost-post-pandemic world.

I have written this book for pastors, physicians, chaplains, seminarians, Christians who work in the medical field, and people in the pew, especially those seeking healing. I have always felt the need to write on theological matters for the body of Christ. Often scholars share useful theological material only with other scholars. This deprives the body of Christ. In my bilingual writing of books and articles, I have tried to reach the pew, where the real need is. Although peer review and scholarship are important, they should not motivate us to ignore the church and its needs. I believe the church must become the beneficiary of the academy's theological assets. The form and style of this book generally conform to that conviction. For the same reason, without assuming that readers in different parts of the world are familiar with the scripture references, I have quoted many of them. I would like this to be a Bible study and an educational reader at the same time.

I am indebted to several friends and colleagues in this effort. Many ORU seminary professors and leaders have informed me and impacted my position on prayer, medicine, and healing. It is hard to document every idea or statement in this work. I was informed and influenced by lectures, presentations, co-teaching, continuing education experiences, and hundreds of informal lunchroom discussions at the City of Faith Hospital and Oral Roberts University for nearly four decades. Prominent among these influencers are the late Drs. Jimmy Buskirk; Gene Koelker; Roger L. Youmans, MD; Howard M. Ervin; Charles Snow; and ORU seminary professors Paul G. Chappell; Robert Mansfield; Edward Decker; Cheryl Iverson; Bill Buker; Tim Ekblad; James Barber; James Tollett; and Paul King.

I wish to express my gratitude to Molly for her support and encouragement which made this book possible. I am grateful to my daughters, Amy and Jamie, for refreshing my memory of the City of Faith project. I am thankful to Renee Chavez, whose editorial assistance was invaluable, and especially to GOODNEWS BOOKS and its chief editor, C. V. Mathew.

I hope pastors will sense a new boldness to pray for the sick as a result of reading this book. I hope believers will pray for the sick in the name of Jesus with increased faith. I hope doctors, nurses, and others who serve in the medical field will find encouragement and see their prayerful work as a vital ministry. I hope sick readers will be encouraged to believe God for their healing in body, mind, and spirit. I would like pastors in training to investigate this topic further with interest and concern. If just one of these goals is realized, I would be more than grateful. With faith, hope, and love, and a prayer for you, the reader, I submit these pages to God for His purposes.

Thomson K. Mathew
www.thomsonkmathew.com

CHAPTER 1

SICKNESS AND HEALTH IN THE HEBREW BIBLE

The Bible opens with the amazing story of God's creation of the universe, with a focus on His work on the sixth day, when He created man in His own image and likeness (Gen 1:26–27), only a little lower than the angels (Ps 8:5). God declared that His creation was good (Gen 1:31). Delighted by the wonder of God's creation and the presence of the Creator, man found himself innocent, healthy, and immortal. According to the Bible, there was no sin in the world at that time and sickness did not exist.

Into this blissful context came Satan in the form of a snake, and temptation, sin, and death followed. The Hebrew Bible tells this story of the fall of humanity and connects sickness and death to sinfulness. It also begins the unfolding saga of God's effort to redeem the fallen humanity culminating later, in the New Testament, with the coming of Jesus the Messiah and His life, death on the cross, and resurrection.

According to Job, the oldest Old Testament book, Satan is the cause of illness: "So Satan went out from the presence of the LORD, and struck Job with painful boils from the sole of his foot to the crown of his head. And he took for himself a potsherd with which to scrape himself while he sat in the midst of the ashes" (Job 2:7–8). In the context of Abraham's lying to the Egyptian Pharaoh about his wife, Sarai (Sarah), illness is seen as punishment: "But the LORD plagued Pharaoh and his house with great plagues because of Sarai, Abram's wife" (Gen 12:17). A similar incident took place when King Abimelech took Sarah as his wife because of Abraham's misrepresentation: "But God came to Abimelech in a dream by night, and said to him, 'Indeed you are a dead man because of the woman whom you have taken, for she is a man's wife'.... So Abraham prayed to God; and God healed Abimelech, his wife, and his female servants. Then they bore children; for the LORD had closed up all the wombs of the house of Abimelech because of Sarah, Abraham's wife" (Gen 20:3, 17–18).

The story of Israel's emancipation from Egypt and the following journey across the Red Sea through the desert confirms the connection between sin and sickness. During this period, leprosy manifested in response to rebellion, snakebites killed scores of people as a result of sin, and the Israelites encountered a plague (Num 16:47). A multitude of maladies afflicted those who were disobedient. God did not abandon these people but provided them with instructions for health maintenance and healing.

King David also connected sin and sickness: "There is no soundness in my flesh because of Your anger, Nor any health in my bones because of my sin" (Ps 38:3). David's life testifies that sin results in sickness. We read about the sickness of the child born from his adultery as illustration: "And the Lord struck the child that Uriah's wife bore to David, and it became ill.... Then on the seventh day it came to pass that the child died" (2 Sam 12:15, 18).

The apostle Paul, a renowned Jewish scholar, explained the connection between sin and sickness to the church in Rome: "Therefore, just as through one man sin entered the world, and death through sin, and thus death spread to all men, because all sinned—For until the law sin was in the world, but sin is not imputed when there is no law. Nevertheless, death reigned from Adam to Moses, even over those who had not sinned according to the likeness of the transgression of Adam, who is a type of Him who was to come" (Rom 5:12–14).

Keys to Health in the Old Testament

Obedience to God's commandments and a life based on the Levitical law are keys to health and well-being in the Old Testament. Living such a life will not only bring healing, but it will also provide immunity against diseases that are common among other peoples and nations. In a place called the Wilderness of Shur, God "made a statute and an ordinance for them [the Israelites], and there He tested them, and said, 'If you diligently heed the voice of the Lord your God and do what is right in His sight, give ear to His commandments and keep all His statutes, I will put none of the diseases on you which I have brought on the Egyptians. For I am the Lord who heals you" (Exod 15:25–26).

In the Old Testament, God is a good God. We learn there that He wants to bless all the people of the world. He said to Abraham, "I will bless those who bless you, and I will curse him who curses you; and in you all the families of the earth shall be blessed" (Gen 12:3). God's will is His children's well-being. Yahweh, the God of the Old Testament, is in charge of life and death. When Moses presented his lack of eloquence as an excuse not to be God's spokesman, the Lord asked him, "Who has made man's mouth? Or who makes the mute, the deaf, the seeing, or the blind? Have not I, the LORD?" (Exod 4:11). Deuteronomy affirms this position: "Now see that I, even I, am He, and there is no God besides Me; I kill and I make alive; I wound and I heal; nor is there any who can deliver from My hand" (32:39). This God who is in charge of good and evil, blessings and curses, is a healer. Jehovah-Rapha is His name. "I am the LORD who heals you" (Exod 15:26), says God, identifying Himself as Israel's true healer.

Jehovah-Rapha gave strict regulations to His people for healthy living. Diet is vital to better health. The diet instructions in Leviticus begin, "Speak to the children of Israel, saying, 'These are the animals which you may eat among all the animals that are on the earth: Among the animals, whatever divides the hoof, having cloven hooves and chewing the cud—that you may eat. Nevertheless these you shall not eat . . .'" (11:1–4). Detailed instructions on good hygiene were also given:

> "If there is any man among you who becomes unclean
> by some occurrence in the night, then he shall go outside

the camp; he shall not come inside the camp. But it shall be, when evening comes, that he shall wash with water; and when the sun sets, he may come into the camp.

"Also you shall have a place outside the camp, where you may go out; and you shall have an implement among your equipment, and when you sit down outside, you shall dig with it and turn and cover your refuse." (Deut 23:10–13)

Interestingly, the concepts of personal hygiene, infection control, and quarantines did not originate with the United States Centers for Disease Control and Prevention (CDC). The God of the Hebrew Bible Himself gave clear instructions for isolation for health maintenance:

"He who touches the dead body of anyone shall be unclean seven days. He shall purify himself with the water on the third day and on the seventh day; then he will be clean. But if he does not purify himself on the third day and on the seventh day, he will not be clean. Whoever touches the body of anyone who has died, and does not purify himself, defiles the tabernacle of the Lord. That person shall be cut off from Israel. He shall be unclean, because the water of purification was not sprinkled on him; his uncleanness is still on him." (Num 19:11–13)

Consider God's instructions for dealing with leprosy: "He who is to be cleansed shall wash his clothes, shave off all his hair, and wash himself in water, that he may be clean. After that he shall come into the camp, and shall stay outside his tent seven days. But on the seventh day he shall shave all the hair off his head and his beard and his eyebrows—all his hair he shall shave off. He shall wash his clothes and wash his body in water, and he shall be clean" (Lev 14:8–9).

The Old Testament highlights the importance of sexual purity. Leviticus 18 contains very elaborate instructions on this matter. The biblical idea is that health is directly related to a healthy lifestyle built on a moral foundation. Healthy life also takes place in community. Social connections and spiritual good standing are important for health maintenance. A community's health depends on the health of its members. Individuals have a moral obligation to care about the community's health. Everyone's well-being depends on adherence to God's instructions revealed in God's Law.

The ideal of well-being in the Hebrew Bible is denoted by *shalom.* The idea of shalom is broader than simply peace. It is peace, harmony, well-being, and wholeness. What is salvation (*soteria)* in the New Testament is shalom in the Old Testament. At the heart of both is right standing with God. Wholeness as shalom is not just peace or healing. It is more than a physical matter; it is a matter of the spirit. Wholeness, or shalom, involves body, mind, and spirit. It also involves God, the Law, and the community. In the language of the New Testament, it involves the Word, the Spirit, and the community of faith.

The Old Testament underscores the importance of a balanced and regulated life. The Sabbath as a vital concept of rest is presented immediately after the creation of man. God the Creator rested on the seventh day of creation, modeling rest as an important and required element of well-being. "And on the seventh day God ended His work which He had done, and He rested on the seventh day from all His work which He had done. Then God blessed the seventh day and sanctified it, because in it He rested from all His work which God had created and made" (Gen 2:2–3). The Hebrew Bible teaches the importance of having a rhythm of life.

Health Maintenance Is Natural and Supernatural

The Old Testament talks about both natural and supernatural healing. There are references to natural remedies, such as healing balms and oil of healing. Supernaturally, snakebitten people who looked to the uplifted bronze serpent received healing. Miriam's leprosy was healed as she repented. The Old Testament prophets ministered healing to people. Elijah healed a widow's son (1 Kgs 17:8–22). Elisha healed a Shunamite woman's son (2 Kgs 4:8–36). Isaiah the prophet healed King Hezekiah, and his life was extended fifteen years (2 Kgs 20:6). This involved the application of natural medication, prophetic (spiritual) intervention, and prayer.

Healing in the Old Testament is not limited to the body, but also to the mind and emotions. God's Word itself is a healing medicine. The psalmist wrote, "He sent out his word and healed them [those who cried out to Him]; he rescued them from the grave" (Ps 107:20 NIV). The books of Psalms and Proverbs speak often about brokenness and healing.

Amazingly, the human body's own mechanisms often restore health. No wonder the psalmist declared to the Lord,

"I will praise You, for I am fearfully and wonderfully made; marvelous are Your works, and that my soul knows very well" (Ps 139:14).

The prophet Isaiah foretold the coming of the Messiah and prophesied that as the suffering servant, He would heal His people. With prophetic certainty, Isaiah spoke about healing in the present tense: "But He was wounded for our transgressions, He was bruised for our iniquities; the chastisement for our peace was upon Him, and by His stripes we are healed" (Isa 53:5). Later, he clarified the messianic anointing: "The Spirit of the Lord GOD is upon Me, because the LORD has anointed Me to preach good tidings to the poor; He has sent Me to heal the brokenhearted, to proclaim liberty to the captives, and the opening of the prison to those who are bound" (61:1). Noticeably, Jesus of Nazareth affirmed and personally incorporated this prophetic word at a synagogue at the beginning of His public ministry (Luke 4:18–19).

The Old Testament anticipated a new age as it began the last chapter of the book of Malachi with these words: "For behold, the day is coming, burning like an oven, and all the proud, yes, all who do wickedly will be stubble. . . . But to you who fear My name The Sun of Righteousness shall arise with healing in His wings" (Mal 4:1–2). The Christian community affirms that these words are about Jesus the Messiah who was to come.

God of the Old Testament a Healing God

The God of the Old Testament is a healer. He prevents illnesses and heals the sick. The Passover testifies of God's preventive care. While the Egyptian enslavers were witnessing the deaths of their firstborns, the Hebrew slaves were being protected by the blood of the lambs they had sprinkled on their doorposts in obedience to God's command. God watches over His people and heals them from all diseases.

The God of the Old Testament is not only a God of justice; He is also a God of mercy who answers prayers. God is almighty. He told Abram, "I am Almighty God; walk before Me and be blameless" (Gen 17:1). He is omnipresent (present everywhere). The psalmist wrote, "Where can I go from Your Spirit? Or where can I flee from Your presence?" (Ps 139:7). God is omniscient (all-knowing). King David sang about this:

> O LORD, You have searched me and known me. You know my sitting down and my rising up; You understand my thought afar off. You comprehend my path and my lying down, and are acquainted with all my ways. For there is not a word on my tongue, but behold, O LORD, You know it altogether. You have hedged me behind and before, and laid Your hand upon me. Such knowledge is too wonderful for me; it is high, I cannot attain it. (Ps 139:1–6)

The apostle Paul exclaimed, "Oh, the depth of the riches both of the wisdom and knowledge of God! How unsearchable are His judgments and His ways past finding out!" (Rom 11:33).

The Hebrew God is both ceaseless and holy: "The eternal God is your refuge, and underneath are the everlasting arms; He will thrust out the enemy from before you, and will say, 'Destroy!' "For I am the LORD who brings you up out of the land of Egypt, to be your God. You shall therefore be holy, for I am holy" (Deut 33:27; Lev 11:45). He is both a God of love (1 John 4:7–8) and a God of providence who is called Jehovah-Jireh. Abraham memorialized this truth following his journey to sacrifice his son, Isaac, on Mount Moriah. There God provided a ram as a substitute for Isaac. "And Abraham called the name of the place, The-Lord-Will-Provide; as it is said to this day, 'In the Mount of the Lord it shall be provided'" (Gen 22:14).

Yahweh Answers Prayers

This Almighty-Omnipresent-Omniscient-Eternal-Holy-Loving-Provider-God answers the prayers of His people. The Old Testament provides a long list of answered prayers:

1. Abraham, a concerned relative, prayed for his nephew Lot. God answered Abraham and saved Lot.
2. Hagar, a desperate mother, prayed for her son's life. God answered and provided for him.
3. Hannah, abused by her dysfunctional family, prayed for a child. God answered her prayer, healed her barren womb, and gave her a son. He grew up to be the prophet Samuel.
4. Moses prayed for his oppressor, Pharaoh, to stop the plague of the frogs. God answered his prayer and stopped that plague.
5. Elijah the prophet prayed before the hostile prophets of Baal and a backslidden people. God answered his prayer and sent fire down to lead the people to repentance.
6. God heard the prayer of King Solomon when he prayed a prayer of repentance at the dedication of the temple.

God heard the king's prayer and fire came down and the glory of God filled the temple (2 Chronicles 6–7).

7. God answered the prayer of a dying King Hezekiah, healed him, and extended his life.
8. Daniel, a diplomat, prayed for deliverance, and God answered his prayers in unexpected ways.

Yahweh Is Unchanging

The Old Testament presents an unchanging God. "For I am the LORD, I do not change," God said in the book of Malachi (3:6). This conviction is echoed in the New Testament letter to the Hebrew Christians concerning Jesus, who is the incarnate "Immanuel"—God with us (Matt 1:23): "Jesus Christ is the same yesterday, today, and forever" (Heb 13:8). This unchanging God of the Hebrews responds to human cries and changes their situations for the better, which includes granting healing to the sick. Look at the examples of dire situations that changed in response to prayers and petitions; these don't involve healing in particular, but they show a God who hears and answers His people, whatever their need:

• Job, to whom God restored everything he had lost after he prayed for his friends: "And the LORD restored Job's losses when he prayed for his friends. Indeed the LORD gave Job twice as much as he had before" (Job 42:10).

• Esther, the Jewish young lady who found herself in the most hopeless situation, committed herself to prayer and fasting along with her kin, and the hopeless situation changed. The Bible uses the most inspiring words to describe her resolve to call on God: "Go, gather all the

Jews who are present in Shushan, and fast for me; neither eat nor drink for three days, night or day. My maids and I will fast likewise. And so I will go to the king, which is against the law; and if I perish, I perish!" (Esth 4:16). Their prayers were answered in the most unexpected way, and she and her people were delivered from extinction.

Even people outside the covenant benefit from Yahweh's benevolence. The best example of this is Naaman, the Syrian commander who was afflicted with leprosy. A Jewish captive girl who served his wife advised him to visit the prophet Elisha to seek healing from the God of Israel. He made the trip but was first offended by the simple instruction Elisha gave him to receive healing—to dip himself seven times in the river Jordan. However, under advisement, Naaman came to his senses, obeyed the prophet, and was healed (2 Kgs 5:1–19). The Old Testament makes it clear that the favor of healing is not limited to the people of Israel. Israel's God heals non-Hebrews also.

God's Presence Is Key to Well-Being

The presence of God with His people is a major theme in the Old Testament. This concept is evident throughout the Hebrew Bible. God was present in the garden of Eden. Naked and ashamed, sinful Adam and Eve hid behind the trees in the garden, but God showed up in the garden, bringing His presence to the lost souls.

Later, God manifested His presence in the wilderness and called Moses to perform supernatural signs to set the people free from Egypt and then to accompany the emancipated slaves to the promised land. During their journey through the wilderness, "by day the LORD went ahead of them in a pillar of cloud to guide them on their way and by night in a pillar of fire to give them light, so that they could travel by day or night" (Exod 13:21 NIV). Men, women, and children were trekking through the desert, facing the dangers of the wilderness from dawn to dusk. God's presence went before them in a visible way.

Once the wandering Hebrews reached the promised land and established themselves, God spoke to King Solomon concerning the temple he was to build: "As for this temple you are building, if you follow my decrees, observe my laws and keep all my commands and obey them, I will fulfill through you the promise I gave to David your father. And I will live among the Israelites and will not abandon my people Israel" (1 Kgs 6:12–13 NIV). Thirty thousand men working for seven years completed the building of the temple. God revealed His presence to the prince, priests, and people on the day of dedication. The chronicler wrote:

> When Solomon finished praying, fire came down from heaven and consumed the burnt offering and the sacrifices, and the glory of the LORD filled the temple. The priests could not enter the temple of the LORD because the glory of the LORD filled it. When all the Israelites saw the fire coming down and the glory of the LORD above the temple, they knelt on the pavement with their faces to the ground, and they worshiped and gave thanks to the LORD, saying, "He is good; his love endures forever." (2 Chr 7:1–3 NIV)

God never abandoned His people. His presence remained with them even when they were disobedient. This story of God's presence and its benefits, including healing, continued, according to the Hebrew writings, especially the writings of the prophets.

God was present with His people to bear them along: "In all their affliction He was afflicted, and the Angel of His Presence saved them; in His love and in His pity He redeemed them; and He bore them and carried them all the days of old" (Isa 63:9). He was there to solve His people's problems so that they did not have to tackle them on their own: "Listen now to my voice; I will give you counsel, and God will be with you: Stand before God for the people, so that you may bring the difficulties to God" (Exod 18:19). He was present to bless them: "Dwell in this land, and I will be with you and bless you; for to you and your descendants I give all these lands, and I will perform the oath which I swore to Abraham your father" (Gen 26:3). His presence supported and consoled them: "Sing, O heavens! Be joyful, O earth! And break out in singing, O mountains! For the LORD has comforted His people, and will have mercy on His afflicted" (Isa 49:13).

God's presence was offered to strengthen, encourage, and remove anxiety from His people: "Be strong and of good courage, do not fear nor be afraid of them [your enemies]; for the LORD your God, He is the One who goes with you. He will not leave you nor forsake you" (Deut 31:6). God's presence gave victory. God said to Joshua, "No man shall be able to stand before you all the days of your life; as I was with Moses, so I will be with you. I will not leave you nor forsake you. Be strong and of good courage, for to this people you shall divide as an inheritance the land which I swore to their fathers to give them" (Josh 1:5–6).

God's presence was a healing presence in the Old Testament. While the Israelites remained faithful to God, He was their protector, provider, and healer. The key to their well-being was their right relationship with God. God not only provided the Law, but He also provided the means to fulfill His requirements of the Law. Israel disappointed God repeatedly, but He kept pleading with them to seek righteousness and peace. His anger did not last long. His mercy was never fully withdrawn. Even during the most trying times of severe discipline, God's desire for His people remained shalom and Sabbath—peace and rest.

CHAPTER 2

HEALING AND WHOLENESS IN THE NEW TESTAMENT

The New Testament documents the life, death, and resurrection of Jesus and records the inauguration of the church and its initial expansion, especially within the Roman Empire. The concept of sin as the root cause of sickness and death is presumed by the New Testament writers. Jesus told the man who was healed at the pool of Bethesda when He found him in the temple later, "See, you have been made well. Sin no more, lest a worse thing come upon you" (John 5:14). The New Testament sees human sinfulness rather than personal sin as the primary cause of disease. For instance, the disciples asked Jesus regarding a blind man whether his or his parents' sin had caused his condition. Jesus answered them, "Neither this man nor his parents sinned, but that the works of God should be revealed in him" (John 9:3).

Healing the sick was a major part of Jesus' messianic calling. He demonstrated that forgiveness of sin and healing of the body were two connected aspects of His redemptive work. When a paralytic was brought down to Jesus through the roof of a house and Jesus audibly forgave the man's sins, Jesus asked the Pharisees who questioned His authority, "'Which is easier, to say to the paralytic, "Your sins are forgiven you," or to say, "Arise, take up your bed and walk?" But that you may know that the Son of Man has power on earth to forgive sins'—He said to the paralytic, 'I say to you, arise, take up your bed, and go to your house'" (Mark 2:9–11). The patient's response proved the connection between sin and sickness as well as Jesus' authority: "Immediately he arose, took up the bed, and went out in the presence of them all, so that all were amazed and glorified God, saying, 'We never saw anything like this!'" (v. 12).

Jesus was a healer of the sick. His healing work was motivated by profound compassion. The Gospels repeatedly mention this motivating factor. Everyone from individuals to great crowds received His compassionate attention. He had compassion on a grieving mother: "When the Lord saw her, He had compassion on her and said to her, 'Do not weep'" (Luke 7:13)—then He resurrected her dead son. Two blind men received Jesus' compassionate touch: "So Jesus had compassion and touched their eyes. And immediately their eyes received sight, and they followed Him" (Matt 20:34). His compassion extended to the multitudes who followed Him: "And when Jesus went out He saw a great multitude; and He was moved with compassion for them, and healed their sick"

(Matt 14:14). He advised a man He had freed from demonic oppression to go home and bear witness to His compassion: "Jesus . . . said to him, 'Go home to your friends, and tell them what great things the Lord has done for you, and how He has had compassion on you'" (Mark 5:19).

Jesus commissioned His disciples to preach, teach, and heal and specifically authorized them to heal the sick and cast out evil spirits: "And when He had called His twelve disciples to Him, He gave them power over unclean spirits, to cast them out, and to heal all kinds of sickness and all kinds of disease" (Matt 10:1). Preaching of the kingdom of God was not limited to oral announcement. Jesus said, "And as you go, preach, saying, 'The kingdom of heaven is at hand.' Heal the sick, cleanse the lepers, raise the dead, cast out demons. Freely you have received, freely give" (vv. 7–8).

Jesus' authority to heal the sick was challenged. He was accused of delivering people under the authority of Beelzebub (a demon), but Jesus claimed the power of God and presented healing and deliverance as evidence that the kingdom of God had come. "But if I cast out demons by the Spirit of God, surely the kingdom of God has come upon you" (Matt 12:28), He said.

When the imprisoned John the Baptist sent his disciples to Jesus with the question, "Are You the Coming One, or do we look for another?" (Matt 11:3). Jesus replied, "Go and tell John the things which you hear and see: The blind see and the lame walk; the lepers are cleansed and the deaf hear; the dead are raised up and the poor have the gospel preached to them" (Matt 11:4–5). The long-awaited Messiah came to inaugurate the kingdom of God, and there were things to hear *and* see to confirm His authenticity and authority. The things people could see to validate His claims included diverse healings: the blind seeing, the lame walking, the lepers cleansed, the deaf hearing, and the dead raised, even as the good news was preached to the poor, just as the prophet had said.

Jesus healed various diseases. Leprosy (Mark 1:42), paralysis (Matt 8:6), fever (Mark 1:30), and speech impediment (Mark 7:32) were cured. Many chronic conditions, including dropsy, were remedied (Luke 13:11; 14:2). The list of maladies is long: "Then great multitudes came to Him, having with them the lame, blind, mute, maimed, and many others; and they laid them down at Jesus' feet, and He healed them" (Matt 15:30). The Gospel writers summarized these disorders in an all-inclusive way. "Then Jesus went about all the cities and villages, teaching in their synagogues, preaching the gospel of the kingdom, and healing every sickness and every disease among the people" reported Matthew (9:35). Mark said, "Then He healed many who were sick with various diseases, and cast out many demons" (1:34). Luke said, "When the sun was setting, all those who had any that were sick with various diseases brought them to Him; and He laid His hands on every one of them and healed them" (4:40).

Chronic Illnesses and Jesus

The medical world divides illnesses into three categories: acute, chronic, and terminal. Jesus healed all three kinds. It is interesting to see His response to chronic conditions considered hopeless by the patients and the community. The world of the chronic patient is small and often filled with fear and hopelessness. Jesus had compassion for these individuals. He helped them do more than cope with the illness.

John 5 tells us about a paralyzed man who had been sick for thirty-eight years when Jesus met him at the pool of Bethesda. The patient was surprised by the visit and the question Jesus raised: "Do you want to be made well?" (v. 6). The man described how he missed the opportunities to jump into the healing water as expected because others kept beating him by jumping in ahead, and only one person was healed each time the water was stirred. The man knew of healing only one way, by jumping in. He blamed himself and others for his predicament. Jesus did not rebuke him. Instead, He said, "Rise, take up your bed and walk" (v. 8). The man did just that. He took up the very mat that had carried him and walked (v. 9).

We read about a woman who had a very serious chronic condition. With an issue of blood, she was in a socially impossible situation, but against conventional wisdom, she touched the hem of Jesus' garment and was instantly healed. Jesus said that virtue had flowed from Him to heal her and acknowledged that she was healed because of her faith. Luke the physician presents the story: "Now a woman, having a flow of blood for twelve years, who had spent all her livelihood on physicians and could not be healed by any, came from behind and touched the border of His garment. And immediately her flow of blood stopped" (Luke 8:43–44). Jesus did not just help the woman cope; He healed her.

Jesus also healed a man with chronic psychological problems who was subject to demonic oppression. When Jesus arrived at the land of the Gadarenes, "there met Him a certain man from the city who had demons for a long time. And he wore no clothes, nor did he live in a house but in the tombs" (Luke 8:27). Luke, himself a medical doctor, described the man's symptoms: "For it [a demon] had often seized him, and he was kept under guard, bound with chains and shackles; and he broke the bonds and was driven by the demon into the wilderness" (v. 29). Jesus rebuked the evil spirits, who called themselves "Legion," and they entered a herd of swine, and the man was healed (vv. 30–33). The spectators "found the man from whom the demons had departed, sitting at the feet of Jesus, clothed and in his right mind" (v. 35). The maniac became a missionary, and "he went his way and proclaimed throughout the whole city what great things Jesus had done for him" (v. 39).

An example of a chronically handicapped person whom Jesus healed was the blind man in John 9. This is the person who had sparked a theological discussion among the disciples regarding the cause of his blindness. They had wanted to know whose sin had caused his blindness. After correcting their theology, Jesus spat on the ground and made clay with the saliva, anointed the eyes of the blind man with the clay, and told him to wash in the pool of Siloam. The man went and washed as instructed and returned with sight to the One who was the light of the world (vv. 1–6).

Mark's version of the commissioning of the disciples includes specific works of healing: "Go into all the world and preach the gospel to every creature. He who believes and is baptized will be saved; but he who does not believe will be condemned. And these signs will follow those who believe: In My name they will cast out demons; they will speak with new tongues; they will take up serpents; and if they drink anything deadly, it will by no means hurt them; they will lay hands on the sick, and they will recover" (Mark 16:15–18). Issues and ailments related to the body, the mind, and the spirit were all of concern to Jesus.

Jesus used multiple methods, but mostly speaking and touching, to implement healing. Luke says, "So when He saw [the lepers], He said to them, 'Go, show yourselves to the priests.' And so it was that as they went, they were cleansed" (Luke 17:14). Of the two blind men, the Bible says, "So Jesus had compassion and touched their eyes. And immediately their eyes received sight, and they followed Him" (Matt 20:34). Jesus also employed unusual methods, such as the use of spit and mud, as noted earlier. Also as seen earlier, Jesus' commissioning words in Mark instructed the disciples to lay hands on the sick. This method and the use of oil were practiced in the early church (see James 5:13–16). There were occasions during the ministry of Jesus when the sick reached out and touched Him and were healed. The most well-known case is that of the woman discussed earlier who had the bleeding disorder (Luke 8:44).

Signs and Gifts

Signs, *wonders*, *works*, and *miracles* are highly significant words in the New Testament. They all relate to the kingdom of God. The healing works of Jesus were fundamentally signs of the kingdom of God. The coming of the Messiah was the beginning of the manifestation of God's kingdom. Signs confirmed this. In fact, the work of preaching with accompanying signs was to continue after Jesus finished His ministry. Mark concluded his gospel by saying that the disciples "went forth, and preached everywhere, the Lord working with them, and confirming the word with signs following" (Mark 16:20 KJV).

According to the New Testament, the kingdom of God represents the rule and reign of God. It is a mystery that has been revealed in the fullness of time. This kingdom had a time dimension, involving the past, present, and future. The kingdom of God came when Jesus came. It will manifest fully someday, as Jesus prayed, "Father, . . . thy kingdom come" (Matt 6:9–10 KJV). We live between the kingdom come and the kingdom yet to come according to Luke's report: "And when he was demanded of the Pharisees, when the kingdom of God should come, he answered them and said, The kingdom of God cometh not with observation: Neither shall they say, Lo here! or, lo there! for, behold, the kingdom of God is within you" (Luke 17:20–21). Healing was an indicator of the dawn of God's kingdom. Perfect healing of all of creation is anticipated at the full manifestation of the future kingdom of God. As for this present, in-between time, the witness of the New Testament is that signs, wonders, and healing can be expected to accompany the preaching of the gospel.

This is not the only avenue of divine healing in the New Testament. While signs and wonders that confirm the preaching of the gospel are for the benefit of unbelievers, those who are already a part of the body of Christ have been given this benefit of healing as a gift of the Holy Spirit. Paul gives a partial list of the gifts of the Holy Spirit in 1 Corinthians:

> But the manifestation of the Spirit is given to each one for the profit of all: for to one is given the word of wisdom through the Spirit, to another the word of knowledge through the same Spirit, to another faith by the same Spirit, to another gifts of healings by the same Spirit, to another the working of miracles, to another prophecy, to another discerning of spirits, to another different kinds of tongues, to another the interpretation of tongues. But one and the same Spirit works all these things, distributing to each one individually as He wills. (12:7–11)

Although one can argue about whether the gift of healing is resident in a person or only operational for the benefit of the body of Christ, according to this passage, healing beyond signs is made available to the followers of Christ as a gift of the Spirit.

This is the position held by the late professor Howard M. Ervin, the Princeton-trained scholar of great repute who was among the founding faculty of Oral Roberts University. His last published work was a concise but definitive treatise on healing titled *Healing: Sign of the Kingdom*. Ervin argued that signs and wonders still follow the preaching of the gospel; they serve as a sign of the kingdom of God and confirm the good news. God does not perform miracles to entertain believers, but as a sign to unbelievers to confirm His word and to give them a foretaste of the kingdom of God. Signs and wonders manifest the power of God's kingdom. Ervin did not encourage believers to seek signs. Instead, he advised that they should learn the principles of the kingdom of God to live as transformed disciples of Jesus as salt and light in the world and expect God's love gift of healing when needed. Ervin encouraged seminarians and pastors to preach the kingdom of God, to teach kingdom principles, and to heal the sick, as Jesus did.

In my foreword to Ervin's final work, I stated:

> Ervin sees healing as a vital part of Jesus' tri-fold ministry of preaching, teaching, and healing. Healing is a sign of the kingdom of God; it manifests the power of God's reign. . . . Signs follow the proclamation of the gospel and they confirm the message of the kingdom of God. Signs are for the unbelievers. Believers do not need signs, but they can receive healing as gifts of love from their Father. . . . According to Ervin, the faith that heals is the faith that saves, and the faith that saves is the faith that heals.[1]

The New Testament uses several words in connection with healing, including *cured* (Luke 2:21), *healing* (Matt 9:35), *made well* (Matt 9:22), and *made whole* (Matt 9:22 KJV), and presents a multidimensional portrait of God's healing work in the world. Healing involves body, mind, and spirit, but all healing is not religious/spiritual healing. The New Testament affirms professional healers. Luke was a physician. Jesus affirmed the role of physicians when He said, "Those

---

[1] Howard M. Ervin, *Healing: Sign of the Kingdom* (Peabody, MA: Hendrickson, 2002), ix. Used by permission of Hendrickson Rose Publishing Group, represented by Tyndale House Publishers. All rights reserved.

who are well have no need of a physician, but those who are sick" (Matt 9:12). Despite the tradition of the two branches of divine healing ministry—one approving medical care and the other opposing it, even militantly—the New Testament supports natural healing work done by physicians (like Luke) and divine healing ministry by believers (like the apostle Paul).

The New Testament, as a witness with integrity, also reports occasions when the sick did not receive healing and even the Son of God could not offer instant healing. Jesus had to touch a man a second time to complete his healing (Mark 8:25). Paul, in his final, highly self-disclosing letter to Timothy, wrote of a man named Trophimus, whom Paul did not heal: "Erastus stayed in Corinth, but Trophimus I have left in Miletus sick" (2 Tim 4:20). To the Corinthians he wrote about his own unanswered prayers regarding what was most likely a malady: "And lest I should be exalted above measure by the abundance of the revelations, a thorn in the flesh was given to me, a messenger of Satan to buffet me, lest I be exalted above measure. Concerning this thing I pleaded with the Lord three times that it might depart from me. And He said to me, 'My grace is sufficient for you, for My strength is made perfect in weakness.' Therefore most gladly I will rather boast in my infirmities, that the power of Christ may rest upon me" (2 Cor 12:7–9). He appears to have meant that grace is even greater than healing.

Faith and Healing

The relationship between faith and healing is often debated. In some circles, people are blamed for not receiving their healing and accused of not having enough faith. This pattern of blaming the victims of illness is not supported by the New Testament.

Faith has been defined as seeing the invisible, believing the incredible, and accomplishing the impossible. According to the New Testament, those who come to God must believe that He is and that He rewards those who diligently seek Him (Heb 11:6). Faith is listed among the gifts of the Spirit, as well as among the fruits of the Spirit (Gal 5:22 KJV; *faithfulness* in the New King James Version), and Jesus related faith to healing on many occasions (Matt 8:10–13; 9:22, 29; Mark 5:34; 10:52). Although He rebuked individuals with little faith (Matt 14:31; Mark 4:40; Luke 8:25), it was generally not in relation to healing. In Matthew 17, Jesus named unbelief as one factor hindering deliverance and recommended fasting and prayer to accomplish it (see vv. 14–20).

The New Testament refers to at least six modes of healing: (1) faith on the patient's part, (2) the faith of those who brought the patient to Jesus, (3) anointing and laying on of hands, (4) confession, (5) casting out of spirits, and (6) the working of miracles. The Bible also presents different depths of faith, such as a measure of faith (Rom 12:3) and fullness of faith (Acts 6:5, 8; 11:24). Faith comes by hearing God's Word (Rom 10:17). It justifies (Rom 5:1), purifies (Acts 15:9), and sanctifies (Acts 26:18). We must live by faith (Rom 1:17), walk by faith (2 Cor 5:7), work by faith (2 Thess 1:11), overcome by faith (1 John 5:4), pray in faith (Jas 5:15), and be healed by faith (Acts 14:9).

Faith is a necessary element for an individual to be healed, but according to the New Testament, the burden of faith is not on the patient; it is on the community of faith. Still, it is important to understand the role of faith in healing and encourage the sick to believe God. Faith pleases God (Heb 11:6). "Everything is possible for one who believes" (Mark 9:23 NIV). "And these signs will accompany those who believe . . ." (Mark 16:17 NIV). However, when the sick person is too weak to believe or lacks faith, instead of blaming the sick, the community should stand in the gap and declare, like the apostle Paul, "For [we] believe God" (Acts 27:25).

As I wrote in Howard Ervin's *Healing*, Ervin believed that saving faith is healing faith and healing faith is saving faith. The faith that heals is not faith in oneself. True healing faith is a gift and a grace. It must be acknowledged that having faith in ourselves is a way of resorting to the flesh. This type of faith is presumption or delusion. It is clear that one is healed by Jesus, not by anything one does. What is really needed is the faith *of* God. God is the source of such faith. Jesus describes this as mountain-moving faith (see Mark 11). Paul included this faith among the manifestations (gifts) of the Spirit listed in 1 Corinthians 12:8–10. This faith is not developed or worked up; it is simply granted and received.

Types of Faith

Charles Farah, former professor of theology at Oral Roberts University, lectured on several types of faith. (He did not call his faith categories "stages of faith," because he felt that they were not in a hierarchy.) The first type is *historical faith*. For example, a person claims to be a Baptist because his grandparents were Baptists, but he possesses no deeper reasons for his claim. Next is *temporary faith,* which is evident in people who become excited about a spiritual experience for a short time and then lose their enthusiasm. Instead of moving from grace to grace, these individuals go from crusade to crusade. The third type of faith is *saving faith.* When a person repents and accepts Christ as Savior, he or she experiences saving faith. The fourth category of faith is called *faith for miracles.* This type of faith is not a gift of God; rather, it is something a person must work up. The fifth type, *gift faith,* is listed among the gifts of the Spirit in 1 Corinthians 12. Gifts are not earned; they are received. Healing is such a gift of grace. The next type, based on the fruit of the Spirit in Galatians, is called *fruit faith.* Farah calls the final type of faith *ministry faith.* He asserts that every believer is given a measure of faith, according to Romans 12, to minister to others in whatever capacity God has called him or her to minister.

According to Farah, faith for healing does not have to be "worked up." It must be received as a grace. All Christians have a measure of faith, and faith even as small as a mustard seed can minister healing. The best type of faith is not faith that simply ministers to oneself, says Farah; it is the faith that makes one reach out to others. This concept holds significant implications for the ministry of healing in the church and community, as it encourages all of us—ministers, believers, and medical professionals—to pray for healing by faith.

CHAPTER 3

JESUS THE HEALER: HIS WORD AND TOUCH

As we noted in chapter 2, Jesus used two dominant methods to heal the sick: speaking and touching. Sometimes He simply spoke, other times He touched the sick, and often He did both. In this chapter, we will examine the prominent passages describing the occasions when Jesus spoke to people and/or touched them to profoundly change them.

God Calls

God speaks to people. The Bible is a record of people who heard God's voice. God calls individuals for His purposes and commissions them to accomplish His will. Abraham is an excellent example. God spoke to Abraham and called him to leave his tribe and homeland by faith. God promised to bless him and make him a blessing to the nations. "When Abram was ninety-nine years old, the Lord appeared to him and said, 'I am God Almighty; walk before me faithfully and be blameless.

Then I will make my covenant between me and you and will greatly increase your numbers'" (Gen 17:1–2 NIV).

Similarly, God called and spoke to Moses. The Israelites were in bondage, crying out to God. Their cry reached heaven, and God initiated a plan to redeem them, beginning with the birth of a child named Moses. After eighty years of Moses' failures and setbacks, God called him through a burning bush. "When the Lord saw that he had gone over to look, God called to him from within the bush, 'Moses! Moses!' And Moses said, 'Here I am.' 'Do not come any closer,' God said. 'Take off your sandals, for the place where you are standing is holy ground'" (Exod 3:4–5 NIV).

God called Samuel, a young boy in training under a priest named Eli who did not know that the young fellow was to replace him to lead a backslidden people. "One night Eli, whose eyes were becoming so weak that he could barely see, was lying down in his usual place. The lamp of God had not yet gone out, and Samuel was lying down in the house of the LORD, where the ark of God was. Then the LORD called Samuel. Samuel answered, 'Here I am'" (1 Sam 3:2–4 NIV).

Elijah was a prophet who heard God's call to return to him a people who were lost to idolatry and living under a weak and corrupt king named Ahab. "Now Elijah the Tishbite, from Tishbe in Gilead, said to Ahab, 'As the LORD, the God of Israel, lives, whom I serve, there will be neither dew nor rain in the next few years except at my word.' Then the word of the LORD came to Elijah" (1 Kgs 17:1–2 NIV). Another prophet, Isaiah, told of how he had heard the voice of God. "Then I heard the voice of the Lord saying, 'Whom shall I send? And who will go for us?' And I said, 'Here am I. Send me!' He said, 'Go and tell this people: "Be ever hearing, but never understanding; be ever seeing, but never perceiving"' (Isa 6:8–9 NIV).

While for a time the good news of Jesus was kept to the Jews only, God called a persecutor of the followers of Jesus, named Saul, to spread the good news to the Gentile world. He testified of hearing the voice of the risen Christ on a journey to Damascus. Luke reported that incident: "As he neared Damascus on his journey, suddenly a light from heaven flashed around him. He fell to the ground and heard a voice say to him, 'Saul, Saul, why do you persecute me?'" (Acts 9:3–4 NIV). Ananias, a disciple residing in Damascus, stated that he had heard the voice of God concerning Saul, saying, "Go! This man is my chosen instrument to proclaim my name to the Gentiles and their kings and to the people of Israel" (Acts 9:15 NIV).

In each of these situations, God spoke to accomplish His great and specific purposes: to Abraham to bless the nations; to Moses to lead a people out of slavery; to Samuel to judge the people; to Elijah to return the people to God; to Isaiah to declare the coming of the Messiah; to Saul to be an apostle to the Gentiles; and to Ananias to minister to Saul. However, God in Jesus often spoke to people to change their situations for the better or to meet their specific needs. There are many examples.

A Word from the Lord

In the case of the woman who was caught in adultery and about to be stoned, Jesus' unexpected word addressed the problem of sin. "When Jesus had lifted up himself, and saw none but the woman, he said unto her, Woman, where are those thine accusers? hath no man condemned thee? She said, No man, Lord. And Jesus said unto her, Neither do I condemn thee: go, and sin no more" (John 8:10–11 KJV). Another unlikely character—a marginalized woman—found the same grace and heard a similar word at Jacob's well. "The woman said, 'I know that Messiah' (called Christ) 'is coming. When he comes, he will explain everything to us.' Then Jesus declared, 'I, the one speaking to you—I am he'" (John 4:25–26 NIV).

Simon Peter heard a word of comfort and direction from Jesus at a crucial moment in his life. After toiling all night and having nothing to show for it, Peter was on the verge of leaving empty-handed when he heard the voice of Jesus: "He said unto Simon, Launch out into the deep, and let down your nets for a draught" (Luke 5:4 KJV).

A similar incident took place at a wedding at Cana where the hosts embarrassingly ran out of wine. Jesus' "mother said to the servants, 'Do whatever he tells you.' . . . Jesus said to the servants, 'Fill the jars with water'; so they filled them to the brim. Then he told them, 'Now draw some out and take it to the master of the banquet.' They did so" (John 2:5, 7–8 NIV). The water turned into wine, and His word met their need.

The feeding of the five thousand was another occasion in which a word from the Lord was sufficient to address a great need. When the disciples asked Jesus to send the hungry people away, Jesus told them, "You give them something to eat" (Mark 6:37).

The disciples in a life-threatening situation in a sinking ship found calm and peace in a word from Jesus. When they approached Him in distress, He "arose, and rebuked the wind, and said unto the sea, Peace, be still. And the wind ceased, and there was a great calm" (Mark 4:39 KJV).

As we have noticed before, a chronic patient who had spent thirty-eight years at a pool was set free by a word from Jesus. Jesus said to him, "Rise, take up your bed and walk" (John 5:8).

The healing of Jairus's daughter also involved the spoken words of Jesus. When Jairus received news of his daughter's death after Jesus was interrupted by a sick woman, Jesus told the distraught father, "Fear not: believe only, and she shall be made whole" (Luke 8:50 KJV). Later, Jesus went to his house, approached the little girl's dead body, and said, "'My child, get up!' Her spirit returned, and at once she stood up. Then Jesus told them to give her something to eat" (vv. 54–55 NIV). In a similar manner, Jesus also raised Lazarus from the dead: "He cried with a loud voice, Lazarus, come forth" (John 11:43 KJV).

Jesus Called by Name

Jesus often called individuals by their names to help them. He is the good shepherd who "calls His own sheep by name and leads them out" (John 10:3). He calls to show His love and to help during crucial times. He called Martha by her name when she was stressed and worried. He called her from worry to peace and rest. "'Martha, Martha,' the Lord answered, 'you are worried and upset about many things, but few things are needed—or indeed only one. Mary has chosen what is better, and it will not be taken away from her'" (Luke 10:41–42 NIV). He called Thomas, who was in distress and doubt, to faith and trust. "Then he said to Thomas, 'Put your finger here;

see my hands. Reach out your hand and put it into my side. Stop doubting and believe.' Thomas said to him, 'My Lord and my God!'" (John 20:27–28 NIV).

Jesus called Peter by his name from disloyalty, discouragement, and desertion to love, faithfulness, and action. "When they had finished eating, Jesus said to Simon Peter, 'Simon son of John, do you love me more than these?' 'Yes, Lord,' he said, 'you know that I love you.' Jesus said, 'Feed my lambs'" (John 21:15 NIV).

Lazarus was called by name from death to life:

So they took away the stone. Then Jesus looked up and said, "Father, I thank you that you have heard me. I knew that you always hear me, but I said this for the benefit of the people standing here, that they may believe that you sent me."

When he had said this, Jesus called in a loud voice, "Lazarus, come out!" The dead man came out, his hands and feet wrapped with strips of linen, and a cloth around his face. Jesus said to them, "Take off the grave clothes and let him go." (John 11:41–44 NIV)

A grieving and distraught Mary at the tomb of Jesus heard her name called by her resurrected Lord. She was called by her name from sorrow to joy and from depression to awe. The dramatic moment is recorded in John: "At this, she turned around and saw Jesus standing there, but she did not realize that it was Jesus. He asked her, 'Woman, why are you crying? Who is it you are looking for?' Thinking he was the gardener, she said, 'Sir, if you have carried him away, tell me where you have put him, and I will get him.' Jesus said to her, 'Mary.' She turned toward him and cried out in Aramaic, 'Rabboni!' which means 'Teacher'" (20:14–16 NIV).

Jesus Touched the Sick

Jesus not only spoke to bring about healing and relief to the sick and afflicted, but He also touched people to make a difference. The word of Jesus brought healing. So also did His touch. We read of crowds wanting to touch Him: "And the whole multitude sought to touch Him, for power went out from Him and healed them all" (Luke 6:19). Mark said that people everywhere wanted to touch Him: "Wherever He entered, into villages, cities, or the country, they laid the sick in the marketplaces, and begged Him that they might just touch the hem of His garment. And as many as touched Him were made well" (6:56). People believed that if they touched Him, they would be healed. This was the case with the woman with the bleeding issue: "For she said to herself, 'If only I may touch His garment, I shall be made well'" (Matt 9:21).

Children were brought to Jesus to be touched by Him:

Then they brought little children to Him, that He might touch them; but the disciples rebuked those who brought them. But when Jesus saw it, He was greatly displeased and said to them, "Let the little children come to Me, and do not forbid them; for of such is the kingdom of God. Assuredly, I say to you, whoever does not receive the kingdom of God as a little child will by no means enter it." And He took them up in

His arms, laid His hands on them, and blessed them. (Mark 10:13–16)

Matthew told the story of the two blind men who were healed by a touch:

When Jesus departed from there, two blind men followed Him, crying out and saying, "Son of David, have mercy on us!" And when He had come into the house, the blind men came to Him. And Jesus said to them, "Do you believe that I am able to do this?" They said to Him, "Yes, Lord." Then He touched their eyes, saying, "According to your faith let it be to you." And their eyes were opened. And Jesus sternly warned them, saying, "See that no one knows it." (9:27–30)

Mark told of the deaf man who received healing by a touch:

Again, departing from the region of Tyre and Sidon, He came through the midst of the region of Decapolis to the Sea of Galilee. Then they brought to Him one who was deaf and had an impediment in his speech, and they begged Him to put His hand on him. And He took him aside from the multitude, and put His fingers in his ears, and He spat and touched his tongue. Then, looking up to heaven, He sighed, and said to him, "Ephphatha," that is, "Be opened." (Mark 7:31–34)

Jesus touched ceremoniously untouchable people to heal them. Lepers were considered untouchable by law, but Jesus touched them anyway: "And behold, a leper came and worshiped Him, saying, 'Lord, if You are willing, You can make me clean.' Then Jesus put out His hand and touched him, saying, 'I am willing; be cleansed.' Immediately his leprosy was cleansed" (Matt 8:2–3). Jesus was not afraid to touch the dead, who were also considered untouchable. According to Luke:

> When He came near the gate of the city, behold, a dead man was being carried out, the only son of his mother; and she was a widow. And a large crowd from the city was with her. When the Lord saw her, He had compassion on her and said to her, "Do not weep." Then He came and touched the open coffin, and those who carried him stood still. And He said, "Young man, I say to you, arise." So he who was dead sat up and began to speak. And He presented him to his mother. (7:12–15)

Jesus Took the Sick by the Hand

At times Jesus took people by the hand and healed them. Recall the occasion when a boy whom the disciples could not heal earlier was brought before Jesus by his father.

> Immediately the father of the child cried out and said with tears, "Lord, I believe; help my unbelief!" When Jesus saw that the people came running together, He rebuked the unclean spirit, saying to it: "Deaf and dumb spirit, I command you, come out of him and enter him no more!" Then the spirit cried out, convulsed him greatly, and came out of him. And he became as one dead, so that many said, "He is dead." But Jesus

took him by the hand and lifted him up, and he arose. (Mark 9:24–27)

Jesus also took the deceased twelve-year-old daughter of Jairus, mentioned earlier, by the hand: "Now all wept and mourned for her; but He said, 'Do not weep; she is not dead, but sleeping.' And they ridiculed Him, knowing that she was dead. But He put them all outside, took her by the hand and called, saying, 'Little girl, arise.' Then her spirit returned, and she arose immediately. And He commanded that she be given something to eat" (Luke 8:53).

Jesus took Peter's mother-in-law who was sick with fever "by the hand and lifted her up, and immediately the fever left her. And she served them" (Mark 1:29–31).

Recall the story of the blind man who was brought to Jesus for healing. Jesus took that man by the hand and even led him out of the village!

> Then He came to Bethsaida; and they brought a blind man to Him and begged Him to touch him. So He took the blind man by the hand and led him out of the town. And when He had spit on his eyes and put His hands on him, He asked him if he saw anything.
>
> And he looked up and said, "I see men like trees, walking."
>
> Then He put His hands on his eyes again and made him look up. And he was restored and saw everyone clearly. Then He sent him away to his house, saying, "Neither go into the town, nor tell anyone in the town." (Mark 8:22–26)

A word from the Lord Jesus was a powerful instrument. His word addressed both sin and sickness. It gave forgiveness, healing, and relief from other troubles of life. His touch also brought healing and deliverance. It is not outrageous for Christians to believe that Jesus still speaks just as He spoke to Saul on his way to Damascus (see Acts 8) because He is still the risen Lord. It is not beyond reason to believe that He still touches people through the power of the Holy Spirit and that a touch of the Spirit can both heal the sick and deliver the oppressed.

CHAPTER 4

THE BIBLE ON HEALING: A SYNTHESIS

In terms of preventing illnesses and treating diseases, the Old Testament provides detailed and systematic instructions to follow. Under the Levitical law, there are several categories of such instructions. It appears that the law concerning the Sabbath was a priority to the Israelites: "Remember the Sabbath day, to keep it holy" (Exod 20:8). Leviticus 11 deals with the law of wholesome diet, with detailed directives on proper eating. The laws and requirements regarding cleansing and quarantine for both prevention and cure are found in Leviticus 15 and Numbers 5. Ethical requirements of personal conduct that are important for maintaining health and preventing sickness are found in Numbers 6.

The health maintenance principles found in the Old Testament present persuasive evidence that it is God's will for human beings to be healthy. For instance, the Old Testament recommends sanitation (Exod 29:14), cleansing (Leviticus 15), isolation (Num 5:4), hygiene (Leviticus 11), dietary regulations (Leviticus 11), and rest (Exod 20:8–11). Health and healing receive significant attention in the Bible: "I will take away sickness from among you," the Lord promised (Exod 23:25 NIV). The psalmist David observed, "A righteous man may have many troubles, but the LORD delivers him from them all" (Ps 34:19 NIV). He later blessed the Lord, "who forgives all your sins and heals all your diseases" (Ps 103:3). "He sent forth his word and healed them; he rescued them from the grave" (Ps 107:20 NIV), he said in a later psalm.

Many Old Testament figures experienced healing, some of whom we have already mentioned briefly. Miriam was healed of leprosy (Num 12:12–15), as was Naaman (2 Kgs 5:1–15); scores of people looked upon a bronze serpent in the wilderness and were healed of venomous snakebites (Num 21:9); and Job received healing from painful sores (Job 42:10–13). The New Testament provides a longer list of healed individuals. Various forms of healing are seen throughout the Bible. Many barren women were healed, and several people were raised from the dead. A cloud of witnesses received healing through the ministry of Jesus. Healing accounts in the Bible did not end with Jesus' ministry either; healing continued throughout the lives of the apostles.

Wholeness

According to the Bible, we were created as whole persons in the image and likeness of God, but sin brought brokenness and separation from God into our lives. God's ultimate plan for fallen humanity is that we would be restored and reconciled to Him. God's will is our wholeness. The very design of the human body suggests that our welfare is important to God. Modern science is amazed at the human body's built-in immune system, which not only prevents illnesses, but also has the capacity to cure injury and diseases.

Wholeness is the opposite of brokenness, which represents the condition of fallen humanity. To be whole is to be in sound condition, well, happy, prosperous, and peaceful. For followers of Jesus, wholeness is received through Jesus Christ as He restores all that was lost due to Adam's sin (Rom 5:17–21; 2 Cor 5:17–21). Jesus came to seek and to save (Luke 19:10), and to "proclaim good news to the poor . . . to proclaim freedom for the prisoners and recovery of sight for the blind" (Luke 4:18 NIV). Humanity's restoration/healing/wholeness was Jesus' mission. While the secular concept of healing can be reduced to a condition without symptoms of illness or disease, the biblical concept represents wellness, balance, and harmony. The Old Testament idea of *shalom (*peace) and the New Testament idea of *soteria* (salvation) both represent wholeness.

Isaiah 53 deals with whole-person health by promising healing for the body, mind, and spirit. Verses 4–6 state, "Surely He has borne our griefs and carried our sorrows; yet we esteemed Him stricken, smitten by God, and afflicted. But He was wounded for our transgressions, He was bruised for our iniquities; the chastisement for our peace was upon Him, and by His stripes we are healed. All we like sheep have gone astray; we have turned, every one, to his own way; and the LORD has laid on Him the iniquity of us all." "By his stripes we are healed" can represent the physical aspect of healing. "The chastisement of our peace was upon Him" can be seen as representing the mental and emotional aspects of healing. "He was wounded for our transgressions" and "bruised for our iniquities" obviously represent the healing of the spirit. Likewise, Isaiah 61 promises a multidimensional wholeness as the purpose of the calling and anointing of the Messiah: "The Spirit of the Lord GOD is upon Me, because the LORD has anointed Me to preach good tidings to the poor; He has sent Me to heal the brokenhearted, to proclaim liberty to the captives, and the opening of the prison to those who are bound" (v. 1).

Jesus healed the sick during His earthly ministry, and He is the same yesterday, today, and forever (Heb 13:8). However, healing of the physical body was not the only concern Jesus had while He lived on earth; He desired to heal all areas of human life—body, mind, spirit, relationships, and every other aspect of life. Paul emphasized this in 1 Thessalonians: "May your whole spirit, soul and body be kept blameless at the coming of our Lord Jesus Christ" (1 Thess 5:23 NIV). Well-being and wholeness are God's will for humankind, and He accomplished this through the life, death, resurrection, and ascension of Jesus Christ. According to the Scripture, God is a good God (Ps 118:1) who is the giver of all good gifts (Jas 1:17). It is significant that healing is listed among the grace-gifts of the Holy Spirit in 1 Corinthians (12:7–11).

The Bible clearly expresses God's intention to heal His people in both the Old and New Testaments. God referred to Himself as the healer in the Old Testament (Exod 15:26). God the healer loved us and gave Himself for us in Jesus

Christ (John 3:16). "Surely he took up our pain and bore our suffering . . . and by his wounds we are healed," wrote Isaiah of the suffering servant (Isa 53:4–5 NIV).

Who Sends Sickness?

Some Christians interpret certain passages (such as Heb 12:4–10) in the Bible to mean that sickness is an instrument God sends to correct and rebuke His children. They use several examples to prove that God sends illness to His children to correct them: Miriam was struck with leprosy. King Uzziah suffered a similar fate (2 Chr 26:19–20). Nebuchadnezzar was driven to madness by God to teach him that "the Most High rules in the kingdom of men" (see Daniel 4). King Herod was eaten by worms because when his people praised him as God, he did not give glory to God (Acts 12:21–23). Note that these were not all followers of the living God. It is true that God created both the snake in the garden of Eden and the "evil spirit from the LORD" to afflict King Saul (1 Sam 19:9 KJV), but it is difficult to find sufficient evidence, especially in the New Testament, to support the position that God inflicts illness upon His children. It is easier to believe that nothing can reach us without crossing the eyes of God, and that the God whom Jesus revealed as Father is not the author of His children's illness; it is His enemy, the devil, and resulting from the fallen condition of the world and the sinful life of humanity.

Demons and demonic activities are not behind every illness. Although demonic attacks can be the root of some illnesses, the Bible implies a diverse set of reasons for lack of wholeness. These include neglect of one's body, unhealthy diet, lack of proper hygiene, lack of personal disciplines, habits the Bible calls work of the flesh, anxiety, and unworthily taking part in the Lord's Supper.

The Willing Healer

Jesus not only healed the sick but also appointed His disciples to minister healing. He considered His healing work even more important than the law of Sabbath. Luke the evangelist/physician gave special emphasis to Jesus' ministry of healing. He recorded several case studies of healings Jesus' followers had witnessed. Although all the Gospels document many accounts of healing, Luke, possibly because of his professional interest, gave detailed descriptions of Jesus' work of healing. His account includes healing of blindness, deafness, fevers, hemorrhage, and arthritis-type disorders.

Jesus was a willing healer. He did not require heavy persuasion to heal, as He saw healing as a sign of the kingdom of God. Jesus as the willing healer responded to the will of the patient. The man at the pool of Bethesda was asked, "Do you want to be healed?" (see John 5:6). He expressed his desire to be healed in a less-than-perfect way and still was healed. The blind beggar of Luke 18:35–43 was asked, "What do you want Me to do for you?" When the beggar expressed his desire to see, Jesus restored his sight.

The Bible mentions several methods of healing, including calling for the elders of the church to anoint with oil and pray (see Jas 5:13–16). Jesus, as we have already seen, ministered healing in many ways. He healed the sick by pronouncing a word (John 5:8), by touching (Matt 8:15), and by praying, as

He did at the tomb of Lazarus (John 11:41–42). Occasionally He used spittle (Mark 7:33) or instructed individuals to act in certain ways (John 5:8). Sometimes He healed individuals who were not physically present but whose loved ones had come to Him for help (Matt 8:10–13).

The Natural and the Supernatural

The early church did not teach that everyone would be instantly healed. While God used the apostles to minister healing to the sick, they themselves were subject to physical infirmities and limitations. For instance, Paul experienced sickness, pain, and discouragement. He was stoned, jailed, shipwrecked, and snakebitten. He was healed from many disorders but not from all. For instance, he stated clearly that his repeated prayers were not answered on behalf of what he called a thorn in his flesh that was sent by the devil to buffet him. Paul was considered a god when he ministered healing but a wretched man when he was bitten by a snake after the shipwreck. Paul was left for dead but walked away (Acts 14:19) and was able to raise Eutychus from the dead, but later he experienced weaknesses in his own body. Tabitha was raised from the dead (Acts 9:40–42), but James, who was martyred by Herod, did not rise from the dead (Acts 12:1–2). Stephen, who was stoned to death for preaching the good news, was not raised from the dead either (Acts 7:59–60). The Bible presents a balanced approach to the ministry of healing.

The book of Acts presents a ministry of healing that integrated both the natural and the supernatural dimensions. Supernatural acts took place to confirm the preaching of the good news, and the natural complemented the supernatural (1 Cor 15:42–44). The New Testament did not offer immediate healing of the body as God's top priority but pointed to the new and glorious bodies believers would receive at the resurrection as the ultimate healing. The writings of Paul and John make this eschatological perspective abundantly clear: "For our citizenship is in heaven, from which we also eagerly wait for the Savior, the Lord Jesus Christ, who will transform our lowly body that it may be conformed to His glorious body, according to the working by which He is able even to subdue all things to Himself" (Phil 3:20–21); "Beloved, now we are children of God; and it has not yet been revealed what we shall be, but we know that when He is revealed, we shall be like Him, for we shall see Him as He is" (1 John 3:2).

We learn that we can have a foretaste of heaven now and can experience healing as a gift of the Holy Spirit but must wait for a future day for the mortal body to experience immortality and the natural body to transform into a supernatural body. The supernatural interventions we now experience are only a foretaste of the fullness of life God has prepared for us. Jesus' words of institution and Paul's counsel concerning the Lord's Supper in his first letter to the Corinthians seem to affirm that the sacraments have a supernatural healing capacity as a foretaste of the heavenly feast yet to come (1 Cor 11:27–32).

Not every believer in the early church expected to be healed or raised from the dead immediately. The natural was allowed to be natural while the supernatural was welcomed as a gift of God. The expectation of the perfect bodies to be revealed at the resurrection was held before the believers always. Supernatural interventions gave the believers hope. It strengthened their faith, but the supernatural was not in competition with the natural. Luke the physician working with Paul the apostle gave us the best model of this combination of the natural and the supernatural in the community of faith.

Untimely Death and Sickness unto Death

There are some references to the possibility of untimely death in the Bible. Being a fool and being full of wickedness can lead to untimely death: "Do not be overly wicked, nor be foolish: Why should you die before your time?" (Eccl 7:17). Jeremiah recorded one incident where the prophet pronounced death on a false prophet and he died within months: "Then the prophet Jeremiah said to Hananiah the prophet, 'Hear now, Hananiah, the LORD has not sent you, but you make this people trust in a lie. Therefore thus says the LORD: "Behold, I will cast you from the face of the earth. This year you shall die, because you have taught rebellion against the LORD."' So Hananiah the prophet died the same year in the seventh month" (Jer 28:15–17).

Abusing the temple of the Holy Spirit, the church, can also have a deadly outcome. "Do you not know that you are the temple of God and that the Spirit of God dwells in you? If anyone defiles the temple of God, God will destroy him. For the temple of God is holy, which temple you are" (1 Cor 3:16–17). Interestingly, this warning was about defiling the body of Christ—that is, the church—as the temple of the Holy Spirit and not about the human body, which was also described as a temple of the Holy Spirit (1 Cor 6:19–20).

Lying to the Holy Spirit can shorten one's life. The tragic end of Ananias and Sapphira proves this (see Acts 5:1–11).

Finally, not discerning the body of Christ and taking part in the Lord's Supper unworthily can result in untimely death: "For he who eats and drinks in an unworthy manner eats and drinks judgment to himself, not discerning the Lord's body. For this reason many are weak and sick among you, and many sleep" (1 Cor 11:29–30).

The Bible strongly implies a category of illness referred to as "sickness unto death" or "illness by which one would die." When Jesus heard about Lazarus's illness, "He said, 'This sickness is not unto death, but for the glory of God, that the Son of God might be glorified thereby'" (John 11:4). Elisha also "had become sick with the illness of which he would die" (2 Kgs 13:14).

A Word About Prayer

The Bible teaches us to pray and gives us clear reasons for praying. First, we must pray because God answers prayer: "Ask, and it will be given to you; seek, and you will find; knock, and it will be opened to you. For everyone who asks receives, and he who seeks finds, and to him who knocks it will be opened. Or what man is there among you who, if his son asks for bread, will give him a stone?...If you then, being evil, know how to give good gifts to your children, how much more will your Father who is in heaven give good things to those who ask Him" (Matt 7:7–9, 11). Second, we pray because all things are possible to those who pray believing: "Jesus said to him, 'If you can believe, all things are possible to him who believes.'

Immediately the father of the child cried out and said with tears, 'Lord, I believe; help my unbelief!'" (Mark 9:23–24).

The Bible presents a God who is able to do all things. He can do above all that we can ask or think: "Now to Him who is able to do exceedingly abundantly above all that we ask or think, according to the power that works in us, to Him be glory in the church by Christ Jesus to all generations, forever and ever. Amen" (Eph 3:20–21). God is able to save, help (Heb 2:18), deliver (Dan 3:29), and heal us.

The epistle of James provides a blueprint for prayer. One can see several types of prayers in 5:13–18: individual prayer (v. 13), united prayer (v. 15), believing prayer (v. 14), intercessory prayer, effectual prayer, and fervent prayer.

Hindrances to Prayer

The Bible gives several reasons why prayers may not be answered. Following are seven of them.

1. *Asking with wrong motives:* "When you ask, you do not receive, because you ask with wrong motives, that you may spend what you get on your pleasures" (Jas 4:3).

2. *Unforgiveness:* "And when you stand praying, if you hold anything against anyone, forgive them, so that your Father in heaven may forgive you your sins" (Mark 11:25).

3. *Pride:* Jesus compared the prayers of the prideful Pharisee and the humble tax collector and pointed out that the tax collector's prayer would be answered: "But the tax collector stood at a distance. He would not even look up to heaven, but beat his breast and said, 'God, have mercy on me, a sinner.' I tell you that

this man, rather than the other, went home justified before God. For all those who exalt themselves will be humbled, and those who humble themselves will be exalted" (Luke 18:13–14 NIV).

4. *Unconfessed sin:* "If I had cherished sin in my heart, the Lord would not have listened; but God has surely listened and has heard my prayer. Praise be to God, who has not rejected my prayer or withheld his love from me!" (Ps 66:18–20 NIV). "But your iniquities have separated you from your God; and your sins have hidden His face from you, so that He will not hear" (Isa 59:2).

5. *Unreceptiveness to God's instruction:* "If anyone turns a deaf ear to my instruction, even their prayers are detestable" (Prov 28:9 NIV).

6. *Ignoring the cry of the poor:* "Whoever shuts their ears to the cry of the poor will also cry out and not be answered" (Prov 21:13 NIV).

7. *Lack of faith* (a major hindrance): "If any of you lacks wisdom, you should ask God, who gives generously to all without finding fault, and it will be given to you. But when you ask, you must believe and not doubt, because the one who doubts is like a wave of the sea, blown and tossed by the wind. That person should not expect to receive anything from the Lord" (Jas 1:5–7).

Effective Prayer

The Bible gives several principles of effective prayer. John the apostle made it clear that pleasing God by keeping His commandments is the key to receiving answers to prayers: "And whatever we ask we receive from Him, because we keep His commandments and do those things that are pleasing in His sight" (1 John 3:22). Agreement in prayer is also important. There is power in agreement. Jesus said, "Again I say to you that if two of you agree on earth concerning anything that they ask, it will be done for them by My Father in heaven" (Matt 18:19). Having harmonious family relationships is another key to effective prayers. Peter's advice to husbands is relevant here: "Husbands, likewise, dwell with [your wives] with understanding, giving honor to the wife, as to the weaker vessel, and as being heirs together of the grace of life, that your prayers may not be hindered" (1 Pet 3:7). In other words, men are to live with their wives in a harmonious way. The fruit of the Spirit listed in Galatians are character qualities (Gal 5:22–23). Developing these qualities helps maintain healthy relationships within the family and outside.

Having God's Word planted deeply in our hearts helps our prayer life. Jesus said, "If you abide in Me, and My words abide in you, you will ask what you desire, and it shall be done for you" (John 15:7). We are instructed to pray clearly and with focus. Many of our prayers are vague, with unspecific requests. Sometimes our prayers come out of a divided heart. What James said about prayer seeking wisdom is applicable to prayers for healing also: "But let him ask in faith, with no doubting, for he who doubts is like a wave of the sea driven and tossed by the wind. For let not that man suppose that he will receive anything from the Lord; he is a double-minded man, unstable in all his ways" (1:6–8).

Contrary to the impression we get from some, God is not Santa Claus. Our worldly pleasures are not God's great concern. James reminded us, "You ask and do not receive, because you ask amiss, that you may spend it on your pleasures" (4:3). However, if we pray fervently regarding our needs and pains while maintaining a reconciled relationship with God and man He will answer: "Confess your trespasses to one another, and pray for one another, that you may be healed. The effective, fervent prayer of a righteous man avails much" (Jas 5:16).

Prayer and Time

Time is a major factor in terms of answered prayers. We live in the ordinary time, which the Bible calls *kronos*. God works in His time, which can be called *kairos*. In terms of fulfilling His purposes in the world, this time can be called "the fullness of time." Matters such as signs, wonders, and miracles happen in *kairos* moments, when God's time intersects with our time. God is always with us in our ordinary time, and yet there are moments of epiphany when His presence is more tangible and manifest. "To everything there is a season, a time for every purpose under heaven" (Eccl 3:1).

Sometimes God's answer is yes. Other times it can be no, and often the answer is "Not yet." When Jesus' mother brought the need of the family at Cana to Jesus, His initial response was a "not yet." "Jesus said to her, 'Woman, what does your concern have to do with Me? My hour has not yet come'" (John 2:4). There are some who teach that repeating a prayer for healing is a sign of unbelief. But the apostle Paul prayed earnestly three times about the thorn in his flesh, which was an attack from Satan, but he did not receive an answer. Instead, he received a word from the Lord saying, "My grace is sufficient for you" (2 Cor 12:7–9).

Praying repeatedly for a healing is not a sign of lack of faith. Paul's experience teaches that one must continue to pray until one receives an answer or hears a word from the Lord concerning the situation. It appears that even Jesus prayed twice on one occasion to heal a blind man (Mark 8:25). After the initial effort to heal the man, he could see men only as trees. But after a second touch, he was able to see everything clearly. Healing can be progressive. Jesus' work with the blind man verifies what Oral Roberts often stated: "God heals instantly, gradually, and ultimately in the resurrection." A literal translation of Matthew 7:7 is relevant here: "Keep on asking, and it shall be given to you, keep on seeking and you shall find, keep on knocking and the door shall be opened to you."

When the answer to prayer is something different from what we expect, we can trust God's will for our lives, recognizing that God's ways are not like ours: "'For My thoughts are not your thoughts, nor are your ways My ways,' says the LORD. 'For as the heavens are higher than the earth, so are My ways higher than your ways, and My thoughts than your thoughts'" (Isa 55:8–9). We can trust that God's ways are better than anything we can imagine. God is a good God who wants the very best for His children, and His will must be our ultimate well-being. When our prayers are seemingly unanswered, we can continue to trust God as Paul did when he faced the thorn in his flesh. We can continue to live by faith, trusting in God's grace, mercy, and provisions. We can be sure that even when we may not see an answer in the form we expect, we can still trust God to meet our needs in His own special ways.

Christian life is a life of gratitude. We are advised to rejoice evermore, pray without ceasing, and give thanks in everything (1 Thess 5:16–18). We can heed the admonition of the apostle, "Be anxious for nothing, but in everything by prayer and supplication, with thanksgiving, let your requests be made known to God" (Phil 4:6). As we pray and praise God with thankful hearts and continue to live by faith in dependence on God, according to the Word of God, He will intervene in our lives by giving us healing or an abundance of grace.

Too Little and Too Much Faith

The Bible makes it clear that faith is required to receive healing. It appears that Christians can suffer from not only having too little faith but also from having too much faith. James taught us to ask in faith (1:6), and Jesus said, "For assuredly, I say to you, if you have faith as a mustard seed, you will say to this mountain, 'Move from here to there,' and it will move; and nothing will be impossible for you'" (Matt 17:20). Paul used the term "a measure of faith" (Rom 12:3). In any case, faith is a requirement of divine healing, and lack of faith can hinder healing. On the other hand, some believers suffer from presumption, which can be defined as "claiming too much faith without having its bearing in the Word of God." Presumption causes some to "name it and claim it." A lack of faith and an "excess" of faith (presumption) can hinder God's healing work.

The apostle John wrote, "Now this is the confidence that we have in Him, that if we ask anything according to His will,

He hears us. And if we know that He hears us, whatever we ask, we know that we have the petitions that we have asked of Him" (1 John 5:14–15). It is better not to substitute faith in the Lord Jesus Christ with some fixed healing formula, a favorite teacher's personal instruction, or faith in one's own faith. It is best to remember that ultimately, we must pray, trusting God's goodness and His will for our lives, knowing that God is a good God, He loves His children, and He wants to bless them. Everything God does in our lives must be seen with an eternal perspective. Learning to live by faith and depending on the grace and mercy of God, we must keep this truth always in our hearts: "the sufferings of this present time are not worthy to be compared with the glory which shall be revealed in us" (Rom 8:18).

Some Biblical Conclusions

Based on a review of the biblical texts, one can draw several conclusions about sickness and health. First, health and illness are both dynamic in nature. Health is not merely the absence of symptoms; it is the wholeness of being. Wholeness is the aspect of human nature that defies fragmentation in body, mind, and spirit.

Second, human beings are unitary. In other words, the human body, mind, and spirit are fearfully and wonderfully interwoven at profound levels. Each aspect of human life interacts with and influences every other aspect, which means that when one part of a person is hurting, he or she hurts throughout his or her body, mind, and spirit.

Third, one's life and lifestyle affect one's wellness. Personal attitudes, habits of discipline, priorities, and choices are significantly related to one's wholeness or lack of health. Healing is enhanced by the things that nourish the spirit, such as love, hope, faith, the will to live, and laughter.

Additionally, God wants us to be whole. Salvation (*soteria*), like *shalom*, connotes salvation, healing, preservation, and harmony in relationships.

God is the source of *all* healing. Whether healing results from faith-filled prayer, natural biological restorative processes, work done by physicians, or a combination of these, all healing—received naturally and supernaturally—comes from God.

It is normative to expect divine intervention in the lives of sick individuals. Although this is not a guarantee of healing for each person in every situation in terms of time and place in this in-between kingdom period, it is appropriate to sincerely pray for divine interventions and to assume that God can and will intervene at any point to bring about the kind of healing He wants. Man cannot thwart the will or sovereignty of God.

As everyone Jesus healed eventually died, all healing is temporary for the believer and takes place in different ways and forms. Sometimes healing comes instantaneously, and at other times it comes more gradually. Sometimes healing comes naturally or because of medical intervention and sometimes as a result of prayer with or without medicine. When no healing is observed, one can say with the apostle Paul, "For I consider that the sufferings of this present time are not worthy to be compared with the glory which shall be revealed in us" (Rom 8:18) and know that ultimately all believers are healed at the resurrection.

Healing is for wholeness, not for perfection. True wholeness, because it involves body, mind, and spirit, is not just about physical wellness, and it results from a Christ-centered life of discipleship. Wholeness involves every aspect of one's life: physical, spiritual, emotional, relational, economic, and environmental.

There is also the reality called the fullness of time (*kairos*). Healing has a time dimension.

The body of Christ is entrusted with the ministry of healing. This responsibility must be exercised with faith (not presumption) and humility (not arrogance) and without promoting false hope. The Christian community is the steward of these healing resources: prayer, faith, sacraments, Scripture, elders, and *koinonia* (fellowship).

Those who accept natural means of healing along with prayer should not be treated as second-class Christians who do not deserve divine help. Blaming the patient for lack of healing is never a good idea.

Healing ministry is an extension of the ministry of Jesus. Inhabited by the life-giving Spirit of Jesus, a Christian can be a "living reminder" of Jesus, as Henri Nouwen would say,[1] and pray for the sick. Motivated by God's love and enabled by His Spirit, a Christian can be a channel of God's grace and an agent of the grace gift of healing.

---

[1] See Henri J. M. Nouwen, *The Living Reminder: Service and Prayer in Memory of Jesus* (New York: HarperCollins, 1977).

CHAPTER 5

FROM PENTECOST TO THE POST-REFORMATION CHURCH

Jesus commissioned His disciples to go to all the world and preach the good news. This commission included a call to administer healing to the sick. He promised them that signs and wonders would follow their ministry. The disciples were called and prepared for this work even before the last stage of the Lord's life on earth: "And as you go, preach, saying, 'the kingdom of heaven is at hand.' Heal the sick, cleanse the lepers, raise the dead, cast out demons. Freely you have received, freely give'" (Matt 10:7–8). Jesus desired that His disciples would heal the sick and promised them that they would do the works that He did, and even greater works than He did, because He was going to His Father (John 14:12). He told them that upon His ascension they would receive the Holy Spirit, who would empower them to fulfill their mission in His absence. The same Spirit that was upon Jesus would be on His followers also.

The First Century

After the ascension of Jesus, His followers who were empowered by the Holy Spirit preached the gospel and ministered healing to the sick. They witnessed signs and wonders confirming their preaching. It is obvious from the introductory statement of the book of Acts that it was Luke's second volume and that in it he was documenting how Jesus was continuing to do His work through His followers. The Gospel of Luke, his original work, was the record of what Jesus *began* to do and teach: "The former account I made, O Theophilus, of all that Jesus began both to do and teach, until the day in which He was taken up, after He through the Holy Spirit had given commandments to the apostles whom He had chosen . . . 'But you shall receive power when the Holy Spirit has come upon you; and you shall be witnesses to Me in Jerusalem, and in all Judea and Samaria, and to the end of the earth'" (Acts 1:1–2, 8).

Luke reported that fear came upon everyone as signs and wonders were done by the apostles (Acts 2:43 KJV). He went on to report what happened in Jerusalem: "They brought the sick out into the streets and laid them on beds and couches, that at least the shadow of Peter passing by might fall on some of them. Also a multitude gathered from the surrounding cities to Jerusalem, bringing sick people and those who were tormented by unclean spirits, and they were all healed" (5:15–16).

The ministry of healing was not confined to the apostles. It appears that ordinary believers were empowered to perform signs and wonders. Acts reported that signs and wonders were performed by both Stephen and Philip. They were members of the community of faith who were originally chosen for the task of serving tables but went on to become public ministers of preaching and healing. Luke tells us that Stephen, before his martyrdom, was full of faith and power and performed great wonders and miracles among the people (Acts 6:8 KJV). Likewise, Philip went down to the city of Samaria and preached Christ, and his preaching was accompanied by signs and wonders: "And the multitudes with one accord heeded the things spoken by Philip, hearing and seeing the miracles which he did. For unclean spirits, crying with a loud voice, came out of many who were possessed; and many who were paralyzed and lame were healed. And there was great joy in that city" (Acts 8:6–8). Simon, a sorcerer in Samaria, was so impressed that he tried to purchase the power he had witnessed (8:18–19).

Later, signs and wonders and healings accompanied Paul's ministry in the gentile world. His conversion itself was a wonder, as a bright light from heaven blinded him on his way to Damascus and an audible voice spoke to him. Concerning his work in Iconium before he had to flee for his life due to resistance and threats, Luke wrote: "Therefore [Paul and Barnabas] stayed there a long time, speaking boldly in the Lord, who was bearing witness to the word of His grace, granting signs and wonders to be done by their hands" (Acts 14:3).

There is ample evidence that the ministry of healing continued throughout the history of the church. The classic works by Ronald A. N. Kydd and Morton T. Kelsey are excellent sources of this history.[1] Additionally, Eddie L. Hyatt has done

---

[1] See Ronald A. N. Kydd, *Healing Through the Centuries: Models for Understanding* (Carol Stream, IL: Tyndale, 1998); Morton Kelsey, *Healing and Christianity: A Classic Study* (New York: HarperCollins, 1976).

extensive research on this topic and has provided very useful documentation in his *2000 Years of Charismatic Christianity.*[2] We will briefly review this history from these and other sources.

The Second, Third, and Fourth Centuries

The persecution of Christians began by the middle of the first century and continued for almost three centuries (to c. AD 320), but there is evidence that the ministry of healing continued even during this difficult period. Justin Martyr, who lived in the second century, wrote that healing and casting out of demons took place during his time by the anointing with oil, laying on of hands, administration of sacraments, and exorcism.[3] Quadratus, from the same period, testified that the continued presence of men in his day who had been healed left no question regarding the reality of physical healing.[4] Irenaeus, second-century bishop of Lyons, wrote about healing by laying on hands and casting out demons and even raising of the dead, which he attested "has been frequently done in the brotherhood on account of some necessity."[5] Ronald Kydd quoted from

---

[2] Eddie L. Hyatt, *2000 Years of Charismatic Christianity: A 21ˢᵗ Century Look at Church History from a Pentecostal/Charismatic Prospective* (Lake Mary, FL: Charisma House, 2002).

[3] R. A. N. Kydd, "Healing in the Christian Church," in Stanley M. Burgess, ed., *The New International Dictionary of Pentecostal and Charismatic Movements*, rev. and expanded ed. (Grand Rapids: Zondervan, 2002), 699 (hereinafter referred to as Burgess, *NIDPCM*); Kelsey, *Healing and Christianity*, 137.

[4] Kelsey, 149; Roger Youmans, *Healing Team Concepts Manual* (Tulsa, OK: Oral Roberts University School of Medicine, 1989), 47. (This book was an unpublished reader that was printed by the ORU Bookstore and required for fourth-year medical students for a course called "Healing Team Concepts.")

[5] Kydd, "Healing in the Christian Church," 700; Kelsey, *Healing and Christianity*, 150.

Irenaeus's *Against Heresies*: "Wherefore, also, those who are in truth [Christ's] disciples, receiving grace from Him, do in His name perform [miracles], so as to promote the welfare of other men, according to the gift which each one has received from Him . . . [Some] heal the sick by laying their hands upon them, and they are made whole."[6]

Hippolytus of Rome, a second–third century theologian, wrote that communion and anointing with oil could bring about healing. His *Apostolic Tradition,* which reflects second-century Christian practices, recognized healing as a gift given by God. "If anyone among the laity appears to have received a gift of healing by revelation, hands shall not be laid on him, because the matter is manifested."[7] His contemporary Tertullian (160–240) wrote about charismatic gifts, such as tongues, prophecy, and healing, and stated that Christians can expel demons and effect cures. He described the joyful Christian life as involving "expelling demons, effecting cures, seeking revelations, and living to God."[8] Gregory of Neocaesarea (213–270), who was called a wonder-worker, performed miracles, exorcism, and healing, according to Gregory of Nyssa.

Origen (185–284) affirmed the ministry of healing. He reported that he had seen many being delivered from serious ailments, mental illnesses, and countless other diseases. According to Kydd, Origen claimed that Christians "perform many cures."[9]

---

[6] Kydd, "Healing in the Christian Church," 700.

[7] Kydd, 700.

[8] Kydd, 699; Kelsey, *Healing and Christianity,* 337–38.

[9] Kydd, "Healing in the Christian Church," 700, Kelsey, *Healing and Christianity,* 151.

Cyprian (200–258), bishop of Carthage, believed that the sacrament of baptism had the power to set a person free from demonic oppression and all its impact.[10] Concerning demonic spirits, he said, "These [spirits] when adjured by us are forced to go out of the bodies which they have possessed."[11] Cyprian did not claim that everyone he prayed for received divine healing. Both R. A. N. Kydd and Roger Youmans wrote about a series of plagues that swept through the Roman Empire during the mid-third century when, although Christians unselfishly cared for the sick, many perished. Cyprian acknowledged this, which makes his testimony of healing and deliverance even more believable.

Basil, one of the Cappadocian fathers, believed in prayer and medicine. He held that medical science is a gift of God to be used when needed but that God heals without medicine. Trained as a physician, Basil is believed to have operated the very first hospital, called Basileias. Healings and miracles took place through Basil's ministry.[12] Gregory of Nazianzus described Basileias this way: "Where illness becomes a school of wisdom, where disease is regarded in a religious light, where misery is changed to happiness, where Christian charity shows its most striking proof."[13]

An approved ministry of healing the sick continued in the church after the Council of Nicaea in the fourth century. In

---

[10] Kelsey, *Healing and Christianity*, 153.

[11] Kydd, "Healing in the Christian Church," 699.

[12] Peter J. Floriani, *An Introduction to the History of the Hospital* (n.p.: independently published, 2018), 21. See Youmans, *Healing Team Concepts Manual*, 49; Kelsey, *Healing and Christianity*, 167.

[13] Youmans, *Healing Team Concepts Manual*, 47.

fact, there was a provision for the ordination of healers in the *Apostolic Constitutions*, a liturgy dated to the second half of the fourth century. Church historian Paul Chappell said, "There is . . . abundant evidence through the early church fathers (e.g., Irenaeus, Origen, Justin Martyr, Tertullian, Augustine) to verify the continued widespread practice of divine healing after the time of the apostles. Pope Innocent I described anointing and prayer for the sick as a right every sick believer should expect."[14]

Healings and miracles took place during the monastic period. For instance, a monk named Palladius described a number of healings, including three that had happened in his presence.[15] His writings included stories of other monks who ministered healing and cast out demons.[16] John Chrysostom (347–407) believed in healing and listed examples of healings he witnessed. He emphasized that the healings were done by God and not by men.[17]

Differing Theologies of the Doctors of the Church

A split happened in terms of the doctrine of healing between the Eastern church and the Western church during this period. The Cappadocian fathers represented the position of the Eastern church on this matter.[18] Basil the Great of Caesarea, his brother Gregory of Nyssa, and their friend Gregory of Nazianzus

---

[14] Paul G. Chappell, "Heal, Healing," in Walter A. Elwell, ed., *Evangelical Dictionary of Theology*, 2nd ed. (Grand Rapids: Baker Academic, 2001), 540.

[15] Kelsey, *Healing and Christianity*, 164.

[16] Kelsey, 165.

[17] Kelsey, 176.

[18] Youmans, *Healing Team Concepts Manual*, 48–49.

believed it was natural for Christians to pray for and to receive healing.[19] Basil believed in miracles and considered miraculous physical healing as something to be expected.[20] He considered healing as a gift of God. To him, healing through miracles was the evidence of God's grace.

It was a different story in the West.[21] The Western church found miraculous healing inconsistent with rational knowledge. It seems that the wealthy and the powerful of the Roman society could not accept the simple teaching of healing practiced by earlier Christians. In fact, many in Roman society looked down on Christians because they expressed brotherly love toward strangers, and especially toward the poor and sick.

Four doctors of the church had great influence over the Western church: Ambrose of Milan, who established the basis for the Roman papacy; Augustine of Hippo, who authored *The City of God*; Jerome, who translated the Bible into the Latin Vulgate; and Gregory the Great, who became one of the most influential theologians on sickness and healing. Ambrose witnessed many healing miracles but saw them as having to do more with spiritual meaning than with physical benefit. Augustine taught that the age of miracles was past.[22] Although the author of *The City of God* later acknowledged that miracles of healing still occurred in his day, the damage was already done.[23] Jerome believed in

---

[19] Kelsey, *Healing and Christianity*, 159–60.

[20] Kelsey, 167.

[21] Youmans, *Healing Team Concepts Manual*, 49–50.

[22] Kelsey, *Healing and Christianity*, 134.

[23] Kelsey, 184.

miracles but did not acknowledge witnessing any.[24] His focus was not the healing of the body. Gregory the Great's book *Pastoral Rule* influenced European thinking on these subjects for at least five centuries.[25] Gregory saw illness as God's testing of His children and as an instrument of God to rebuke and correct them. Christians must endure God's chastisement patiently, he taught. He also attributed specific illnesses to particular sins and proposed corresponding penances for cure.

These theological positions expressed themselves in the liturgy of the Western church.[26] While the Eastern church maintained the oldest meaning of the sacramental acts of the church, such as anointing with oil, laying on of hands, and praying for healing, the Western church neglected these or provided different meanings. It was seen that the patient endurance of suffering administered by God was more important than expecting or receiving healing.[27] Self-denial and self-inflicted pain became virtues. The influence of the doctors of the church established this transition.

Middle Ages

Healing ministry continued during the Middle Ages. Unfortunately, the simplicity of the healing ministry of the biblical days and the first centuries of the church was lost during this period. "In the sixth century, Gregory the Bishop of Rome saw illness as a scourge of God. This teaching moved

---

[24] Kelsey, 191.
[25] Kelsey, 196.
[26] Youmans, *Healing Team Concepts Manual*, 51.
[27] Kelsey, 198.

the western church into turmoil and confusion during the seventh and eight centuries," said Jacob Muthalali, who wrote on this subject based on his doctor of ministry research project completed at Oral Roberts University.[28]

Kydd identified the following changes.[29] Anointing with oil and prayer were replaced with the ritualistic use of specially consecrated oil. Other practices, such as the use of healing objects, entered the church's ministry. Devotional objects of healing were provided to the sick, and shrines of the martyrs were established. As the sacrament of healing morphed into the last rites, healing of the body was eclipsed by the well-being of the soul. A belief developed that God causes illness to purify the soul.[30] Influenced by Greek philosophy, the church saw the body as a hindrance to spiritual growth.[31]

Paul Chappell noted the decline in healing ministry: "By the ninth century a significant decline in the practice of divine healing had begun."[32] It appears that the institutionalized church spiritualized the ministry of healing and made the wrath of God more obvious than His love.

During the period called the Dark Ages, from the fifth to the tenth century, paganism and superstitions grew and the picture of an angry God became more obvious than that of a healing Jesus. As the church placed its hopes in the saints and other intermediaries between God and man, the Dark Ages

---

[28] Jacob Muthalali, *Heal the Sick in the Name of Jesus Christ* (n.p., 2006), 33.

[29] Kydd, *International Dictionary*, 702–8.

[30] Muthalali, *Heal the Sick in the Name of Jesus Christ*, 33–34.

[31] Youmans, *Healing Team Concepts Manual*, 54.

[32] Chappell, "Heal, Healing," 540.

became a long season of despair. During this period, which is arguably considered a long season of cultural and intellectual decline, as healing became intertwined with superstition, the monasteries became places of prayer and care for people who were poor, sick, and afflicted. The compassionate work of monks kept the ministry of healing alive.[33]

The number of approved sacraments varied throughout the first millennium of the history of the church. By the twelfth century, church leaders decided upon seven as the exact number of sacraments. Anointing of the sick was one of them.[34] By then unfortunately, the sacrament became *extreme unction*, and in the West, its focus had become forgiveness of sin and death, not healing. Previously the sacrament was known as the *holy oil, the unction of the sick*, the *blessing of consecrated oil*, and *unction of God*[35] and in most cases available only to those who were rich and powerful.[36] *The Catholic Encyclopedia* defines extreme unction as "a sacrament of the New Law instituted by Christ to give spiritual aid and comfort and perfect spiritual health, including, if need be, the remission of sins, and also, conditionally, to restore bodily health, to Christians who are seriously ill; it consists essentially in the unction by a priest of the body of the sick person, accompanied by a suitable form of

---

[33] Youmans, *Healing Team Concepts Manual*, 51–52. *See also* Floriani, *An Introduction to the History of the Hospital*, 25.

[34] *Encyclopedia Britannica*, s.v. "anointing of the sick," accessed August 22, 2022, https://www.britannica.com/topic/anointing-of-the-sick.

[35] Patrick Toner, "Extreme Unction," *The Catholic Encyclopedia*, vol. 5. (New York: Robert Appleton, 1909), http://www.newadvent.org/cathen/05716a.htm.

[36] Joshua J. Mark, s.v. "The Medieval Church," *World History Encyclopedia*, June 17, 2019, https://www.worldhistory.org/Medieval_Church/.

words," but concludes, "Theologians are agreed that extreme unction may in certain circumstances be the only, and therefore the necessary, means of salvation for a dying person."[37]

Thomas Aquinas (1225–1274), the highly influential theologian who believed in a rational cause-and-effect approach to the workings of nature, cemented the intellectual position against divine healing in the West. He considered God's natural laws perfect, with no room for the supernatural in the natural realm.[38] The natural world operates on God-ordained laws, which are fixed and nonnegotiable. Nothing authentic happens outside the predictable realm of a nature created to function within fixed laws. In this thinking, "there was no need for God to break through to the lives of men," said Morton Kelsey.[39] Even during this period of naturalism, the monasteries continued to offer refuge to the sick and the poor.

The Pre-Reformation Period

Healing ministry, despite deviations from its biblical norms, continued throughout the Middle Ages. Before the Reformation, several groups were well-known for their teaching and practices of healing and miracles. A collection of such groups was called Cathari (1000–1300). They were condemned by the Catholic Church and persecuted.[40] A second group, called the Waldenses, of the twelfth century was also known for their

---

[37] Toner, "Extreme Unction."

[38] Kelsey, *Healing and Christianity*, 204; Youmans, *Healing Team Concepts Manual*, 52.

[39] Kelsey, *Healing and Christianity*, 205.

[40] O. G. Oliver, "Cathari," in Walter A. Elwell, ed., *Evangelical Dictionary of Theology*, 2nd ed. (Grand Rapids: Baker Academic, 2001), 214.

practice of healing and miracles.[41] They traced their roots to the first-century apostolic church. Believing in the authority of the Scripture, they allowed lay members to preach and minister and practiced praying for the sick, according to James 5:14–15. "During the pre-Reformation period," wrote Chappell, "the practice of healing continued, but only in isolated instances, as with Bernard of Clairvaux, or the Waldensians."[42]

Historians have traced the story of healing during the Reformation. Even though the church had lost its way in terms of biblical teaching and allowed superstitions to enter, the church's tradition of healing ministry continued. Experts have speculated that the entrance of superstition into the healing practices during the Dark Ages was one of the reasons this ministry was marginalized. Martin Luther did not believe in divine healing initially but prayed for the sick later in his ministry. He "believed that many physical illnesses originated in mental causes such as fear, sin and stress," said Muthalali.[43] "Luther and the English Reformers renewed the practice in their ministries," added Chappell.[44]

According to Eddie Hyatt, who has served as a pastor and theological educator in North America, the Anabaptists, contemporaries of Martin Luther, practiced praying for the sick.[45] As Luther restored the idea of the priesthood of all believers, Hyatt said, the Anabaptists restored the idea of

---

[41] Chappell, "Heal, Healing," 540.
[42] Chappell, 540.
[43] Muthalali, *Heal the Sick in the Name of Jesus Christ*, 34.
[44] Chappell, "Heal, Healing," 540.
[45] Hyatt, *2000 Years of Charismatic Christianity*, 77, 83.

prophethood of all believers, as they believed that every Christian was empowered by the Holy Spirit to perform healings and miracles. Interestingly, during this period, the use of medicine remained a matter of choice. Some groups endorsed it. Others considered it unnecessary or even wrong.[46]

The Post-Reformation Period

The Protestant reformers of the sixteenth century were followers of Thomas Aquinas's thinking, that healing miracles and other gifts had ceased in the church.[47] John Calvin wrote, "But the gift of healing disappeared with the other miraculous powers which the Lord was pleased to give for a time, that it might render the new preaching of the gospel for ever wonderful. Therefore, even were we to grant that anointing was a sacrament of those powers which were then administered by the hands of the apostles, it pertains not to us, to whom no such powers have been committed."[48] Martin Luther was of similar disposition but reversed his position later, as Augustine had done. Luther acknowledged contemporary miracles of healing. The Quakers also believed in divine healing and practiced praying for the sick. Yet, despite exceptions, cessationist thinking prevailed in the Reformed church for a long time, and a renewed theology and practice of healing ministry did not become a major concern until the dawn of the Wesleyan Holiness revival of the eighteenth century. Beginning with the

---

[46] Kelsey, *Healing and Christianity*, 210–11.

[47] Youmans, *Healing Team Concepts Manual*, 54.

[48] John Calvin, *Institutes of the Christian Religion* (Louisville: Westminster John Knox Press, 1960), bk. IV, chap. 19, 18.

Wesleyans, the pre-Pentecostal Holiness movement, with its theological focus on sanctification, became the cradle for the emerging theology and ministry of divine healing.

The early Methodists believed in prayer and healing. John Wesley bore witness to healings that took place instantaneously in response to prayer. According to Hyatt, Wesley answered his critics in no uncertain terms. He replied, "As it can be proved by abundance of witnesses that these cures were frequently (indeed almost always) the instantaneous consequences of prayer, your inference is correct."[49]

The Great Awakening in colonial America witnessed divine healing. The healing of Mary Wheeler of Plainfield, Connecticut, who was struck down by a "wasting fever," became a major event of this revival in New England. According to historian Kerry E. Irish, "The clear healing of Mary Wheeler helped energize the awakening in New England. It also raised a theological storm. The reformed faith of the Puritan fathers held that miraculous healing ended with Apostolic age. Did the resumption of miracles signify the end of history? Was the second coming of Christ near? Of course, those opposed to the revival and its methods sneered at this display of gullibility by the evangelicals."[50]

The Second Great Awakening, which began around 1796 and continued for at least twenty years, also witnessed spiritual

---

[49] Hyatt, *2000 Years of Charismatic Christianity*, 108.

[50] Kerry E. Irish, "The Great Awakening and the Coming of the American Revolution," *Faculty Publications– Department of History and Politics* (2022), 100, https://digitalcommons.georgefox.edu/cgi/viewcontent.cgi?article=1099&context=hist_fac.

manifestations, including healing, especially among those who emphasized the Wesleyans' doctrine of sanctification. The Baptists and Presbyterians were among those who were impacted by this revival.

The nineteenth-century Holiness movement witnessed both saving of souls and healing of bodies. Although this revival began among the Methodists, it soon spread to other denominations as well, especially within the "higher life" segment of the Holiness movement. Phoebe Palmer of New York City, a notable pioneer of healing ministry in the United States, was a prominent Methodist. The healing movement of the twentieth century within the Pentecostal/charismatic movement owes much to the intercontinental Holiness movement. This impactful movement deserves a closer look.

CHAPTER 6

HEALING AND THE
HOLINESS MOVEMENT

Paul G. Chappell, who served as dean of the College of
Theology and Ministry at Oral Roberts University before
me (he hired me as a faculty member nearly four decades ago),
is a prominent authority on the history of divine healing movements from the eighteenth through the twentieth centuries.
His doctoral research at Drew University is a gold mine of
information on the historical and theological development of
divine healing within the Holiness movement and its incorpora-
tion into the Pentecostal/charismatic movement.[1]

---

[1] I am indebted to Dr. Paul G. Chappell's doctoral dissertation at Drew
University and his lectures at Oral Roberts University (ORU) for the chapters
related to the history of healing within the Holiness movement. A 364-page
unpublished book version of Chappell's dissertation, titled *Great Things He
Hath Done: Origins of the Divine Healing Movement in America* (printed by
the ORU Bookstore), has served as a course reader at Oral Roberts University.
An 18-page journal article based on his research on the origins of the healing
movement is available for download. Paul G. Chappell, "Origins of the Divine
Healing Movement in America," *Spiritus: ORU Journal of Theology* 1, no. 1,
article 3 (1985), https://digitalshowcase.oru.edu/spiritus/vol1/iss1/3.

According to Chappell, one of the earliest groups to promote divine healing was the Society of Friends.[2] George Fox, the founder of the Quakers, practiced praying for the sick as he traveled through the United States. He reported the physical healing of many who attended his meetings. This practice continued among his followers into the nineteenth century. The Brethren, a persecuted religious group that migrated from Germany to America during the 1700s, also believed in divine healing based on James 5:14–15. The historical records of the Brethren include many testimonies of healing through prayer.

The Mormons, founded by Joseph Smith, practiced divine healing too, said Chappell.[3] Smith reportedly sent anointed handkerchiefs to the sick for their healing. Ellen White, one of the cofounders of the Seventh-day Adventists, was a strong advocate of divine healing. She traveled through western New York and New England, offering prayers for the sick. She anointed people with oil and laid hands on them according to James 5:14–15. Initially she thought that medical assistance was a denial of faith in God for healing but changed her position and began to focus on preventive health habits and the practice of medicine. She opened a sanitarium in Battle Creek, Michigan, to practice medicine from a preventive perspective. Later, a medical school was established at Loma Linda University to train doctors in preventive medicine, deemphasizing healing by prayer and faith.[4]

---

[2] Chappell, *Great Things He Hath Done*, 12.
[3] Chappell, *Great Things He Hath Done*, 16.
[4] Youmans, *Healing Team Concepts Manual*, 23–25 (see chap. 5, n. 4).

Healing Roots in Europe

The practice of divine healing in the United States was strongly influenced by personalities and ministries in Europe. Edward Irving, a Scottish clergyman, was a pioneer of emphasizing divine healing and other supernatural manifestations of the Holy Spirit.[5] By 1830, his congregation was experiencing supernatural healings and speaking in other tongues. Irving believed in both medicine and prayer. He founded the Catholic Apostolic Church in 1830 and propagated the ideas of speaking in tongues and divine healing.

The American church received inspiration from Germany also. Johann Blumhardt was a Lutheran pastor in Germany serving in the Black Forest area. He began a healing ministry.[6] Believing the words of Mark 16:18, "They will lay hands on the sick, and they will recover," he prayed for a dying young girl, Katarina, and she was healed. This began a revival as people flocked to his church, confessing their sins and seeking deliverance and healing. The news spread across Europe, and sick people seeking prayers from near and far were brought to his place. Though the church authorities ordered Blumhardt to stop praying for the sick, he continued the practice and in 1852 left the Lutheran Church to establish a faith home at the famous Bad Boll, a former gambling place. That facility could accommodate 150 patients at a time. He taught that sickness was the result of sin and came from the devil. He believed that forgiveness of sin and healing are interrelated and that, in

---

5 Chappell, *Great Things He Hath Done*, 24.
6 Kydd, "Healing in the Christian Church," 701.

praying for the sick, Christians are cooperating with God by exercising faith in Him and praying for the elimination of evil.[7]

Blumhardt thought that there could be no healing unless there was believing contact of the sick person's spirit with God. In other words, one must examine oneself and confess one's secret sins. He also believed that God healed without the aid of medicine or physicians since healing was provided in the atonement.[8] He never insisted that people should give up medicine but believed that healing could take place without the laying on of hands or any physical contact. Blumhardt prayed for many people by means of letters and telegraphs.

Dorothea Trudel was another European who impacted the American healing movement.[9] In Mannedorf, a Swiss village, Trudel prayed for her coworkers who were afflicted with a disease that resisted all medical treatments. They were instantly healed, and that began her healing ministry. Her ministry became well-known, and people from all over Europe came to Mannedorf, seeking her prayers. The demand was so high that she opened several faith homes. Her ministry assistant, Samuel Zeller, became her successor.

Trudel had the distinction of being the first person who was charged with practicing the healing art without a license.[10] This incident took place in 1856. She was ordered to close her faith home and was fined. Trudel complied but reopened the home in 1861. She was sued again after the death of two

---

[7] Chappell, *Great Things He Hath Done*, 28–30.
[8] Chappell, 31.
[9] Chappell, 32.
[10] Chappell, 34.

patients in her facility. She lost the case, but on appeal to the Zurich tribunal of justice, she was acquitted of all charges because, although she did not have doctors at her facility, she allowed the residents to be treated by their own physicians and there were undeniable healings taking place at the home. This trial gave great publicity to Trudel's ministry, and multitudes of people sought her prayers. Many had to be turned away. She also used written letters to pray for the sick. Letter writing became an additional way to extend her healing ministry.

Samuel Zeller laid hands on Otto Stockmayer and prayed for him in 1867, and he was healed. Several years later, Stockmayer opened his own healing home in Switzerland, following Trudel's model. He was a regular participant in the early Keswick conventions that introduced him to participants from both Britain and the United States. He provided the first comprehensive theological foundation for the emerging divine healing movement.[11] The author of the book *Sickness and the Gospel,* Stockmayer was considered the first articulator of the theological position that connects healing to the atonement. He held that divine healing was a vital part of God's work of redemption, basing his teaching on Isaiah 53:4, and believing that Jesus Christ carried both our physical and our spiritual sufferings at the cross of Calvary. Since Christ had carried them on the cross for them, human beings no longer need to suffer sickness and disease.

Stockmayer believed that the sick could receive their healing by faith just as they could receive the forgiveness of sin. He

---

[11] Chappell, 37.

taught that the gift of healing belonged to the church and not to the individuals ministering to the sick. He saw divine healing as a ministry related to the work of evangelism and believed that the power to heal was initially given to the apostles, who passed it on to the elders of the church according to James 5:16, and was then made available to all righteous persons who would fervently pray for the sick. Now all God's people can pray for one another for healing. Since the prayer of a righteous person brings forth healing, sanctification is the most important issue.[12] Stockmayer's theological construct was of utmost importance in the development of the divine healing movement around the world.

This emphasis on the importance of sanctification made the Holiness movement a natural cradle for the development of divine healing ministries. Divine healing was seen as a natural manifestation proceeding from complete sanctification. Holiness teachers believed that perfection, or entire sanctification, was a second and separate work of grace that happened instantaneously by the supernatural work of God. John Wesley considered it a definite experience but believed there was a process of growth and development. Some within the divine healing movement insisted that healing always occurred instantaneously, and any lack of healing was evidence of a lack of faith or the presence of sin in the sick person's life. The Keswick branch of the Holiness movement adapted a progressive sanctification model. They thought there was an instant receival of healing at the beginning of a process of

---

[12] Chappell, 40.

healing but that the patient may still experience symptoms. This meant that God answers prayer for healing immediately, but the actual manifestation of healing may happen gradually.

American Pioneers

Phoebe Palmer and colleagues insisted that entire sanctification is immediate salvation. As healing proceeds out of sanctification, healing also is instantaneous. She taught that one is able to receive sanctification just as soon as one comes believingly. Any delay would not be on God's part, but on the sick person's part. By the 1850s, Palmer had begun to call Christian perfection the "baptism with the Holy Ghost," "baptism with fire," and "Pentecostal baptism." According to Paul Chappell, she was the first person to popularize the terminology "baptism of the Holy Spirit."[13] When Christian perfection was seen as the baptism of the Holy Spirit, available to all believers, it became connected to the gifts of the Holy Spirit, such as divine healing. Accordingly, Christian perfection, or baptism of the Holy Spirit, purifies believers from sin, endues them with power, allows them to live a holy life, and enables them to experience supernatural gifts of God, including divine healing. Chappell established a close connection between the Holiness and divine healing movements and between the European and American healing movements. They were all proponents of Christian perfection.

Ethan O. Allen is considered the father of the divine healing movement in America.[14] He formally associated

---

[13] Chappell, 54.
[14] Chappell, 62.

the doctrine of Christian perfection with divine healing and believed sin is the cause of sickness and that Christ's atonement provided not only for justification but also for purification or sanctification, which would remove illnesses. Like Stockmayer, Allen had been divinely healed. Following his healing from consumption by prayer in 1846, he began to pray for the sick and became the first American to make divine healing ministry his full-time vocation.

Without any special training in praying for the sick as a ministry and informed only by what he read in the New Testament, Allen entered his new ministry. He ministered primarily among the poor and marginalized. He was able to spread his message despite a shy personality by visiting poorhouses, local churches, and faith homes. Though his lack of schooling was a hindrance to his ministry, he traveled throughout the eastern half of the United States for half a century, praying for the sick and teaching divine healing.

Allen influenced a number of people who entered faith healing ministry. Mrs. Elizabeth Mix of Connecticut was one of them. She had been healed of tuberculosis under his ministry. A well-educated and articulate person, and trained by Allen, Mix became the first black healing evangelist in America. She was so highly respected that even physicians sent their patients to her for her prayers.[15] She instructed the sick to pray and then to act upon their faith. She told them not to be concerned about the time between the prayer and the actual disappearance of symptoms.

---

[15] Chappell, 64.

Although Allen made significant contributions to the divine healing movement in the United States, the person who contributed the most to the development of the healing movement was Charles Cullis, a physician in Boston.[16] He served as a link between the Holiness and divine healing movements by successfully convincing prominent Holiness leaders that full salvation included not only salvation of the soul but also healing of the physical body. Leaders of the Higher Life movement influenced by Cullis included A. J. Gordon, founder of Gordon College in Massachusetts; and A. B. Simpson, founder of the Christian and Missionary Alliance (CMA) denomination.

Cullis founded a publishing firm, the Willard Tract Repository, which was the first press in the United States to regularly publish divine healing materials. He founded a faith healing home, conducted weekly healing services in his local church, and held faith healing conventions across the country. He never gave up his medical profession but became the most important person in terms of the history of the divine healing movement in America.

Following a spiritual encounter at a session of Phoebe Palmer's Tuesday meeting for the promotion of holiness in New York City, Cullis experienced sanctification and dedicated his life to taking the gospel of love and care to the poor, hopeless, and neglected people of society. Seeing that the hospitals and even the poorhouses of his day did not offer admission to the indigent who were suffering from consumption, he opened a

---

[16] Chappell, "Heal, Healing," 540. See details in Chappell, *Great Things He Hath Done*, 71–125.

home for such victims so they could receive proper medical and spiritual care. His first consumptives home, where he offered free residence and medical care, opened in 1864. His ministry grew to become a mega-charitable organization that included a school of nursing, a publishing division, several churches, a high school, a Bible college, two orphanages, a home for women in crisis, and a home for the mentally ill. He also opened a college and an orphanage for black people in the South, called the Boytown Institute. Other ministries included outreaches to the Chinese and Jewish people in America. Cullis also sent missionaries to India and South Africa. The focus of all his ministries was divine healing.

Cullis was profoundly influenced by reading the life story of Dorothea Trudel, which convinced him that healing through the prayer of faith is a permanent privilege of God's people. He made a trip to Europe in 1873 and visited the healing works of Blumhardt, Trudel, and George Muller, and began to conduct annual faith conventions in Framingham, Massachusetts, and later in Maine. These conventions emphasized the teachings of Christian perfection but now included the doctrine of divine healing. They became international conferences, attracting significant attention from both the secular and the religious presses across the United States. Divine healing became a matter of concern and discussion in the churches and in society at large during this period. Although he was not a clergyman, Cullis was a tremendous influence on the leadership of the Holiness movement concerning faith healing.

Seeing the success of his local efforts, Cullis began to hold conventions throughout the country in cities such as

Philadelphia, Baltimore, New York, Chicago, Boston, Pittsburgh, and Detroit. They were most effective in ministering healing to the sick and spreading the message of divine healing.

Many books on divine healing were written and published during this period. William Boardman's *The Lord That Healeth* was one highly influential volume published during this time. Broadman was one of the leaders of the Keswick holiness movement. A. J. Gordon's *The Ministry of Healing: Miracles of Cure in All Ages*, published in 1882, also was a landmark publication. Gordon traced the history of the doctrine of faith healing from the early church fathers through the post-Reformation period. *The Atonement for Sin and Sickness; or, A Full Salvation for Soul and Body*, written by the historian of the healing movement, Kelso Carter, became the leading treatise defending divine healing. His volume established that the atonement provided healing for the body and for the soul. He taught that the atonement cleansed all traces of the fallen condition, including sickness, which was considered a result of man's sin and sent from the devil. The vicarious atonement of Christ is the answer to all consequences of sin, including sickness. Another significant publication defending divine healing was R. L. Marsh's *Faith Healing: A Defense*, originally a bachelor of divinity thesis at Yale Divinity School. These writings gave a theological foundation to the experiential work of the faith healers of the nineteenth century.

Cullis influenced other notable leaders of the Holiness movement to provide theological and practical leadership for the movement. William Boardman was the most important person in this group.[17] Boardman's writings argued that the baptism of the Holy Spirit was not a gift conferred upon a selected few but was a gift for all believers that allowed them to receive benefits for the soul and body. Boardman's writings presented Jesus Christ as the Savior who forgives sins, the deliverer from the power of sin, the sanctifier of the human heart, and the deliverer from all the consequences of sin, including sickness. He emphasized that divine healing, like salvation and sanctification, is the ongoing work of the church of Jesus Christ. Divine healing is not just a part of signs and wonders provided for special times but is God's permanent provision for His people according to James 5:14–15. Boardman opened a faith home named Bethshan in London in 1882. Healing services were held there several days a week to instruct the sick in the doctrine of divine healing. Bethshan did not provide medical care to the sick.

In 1885, an international conference of divine healing was held in the great agricultural hall of London, England, led by William Boardman.[18] This meeting brought together the most significant proponents of divine healing of the day to share their knowledge and experiences on this subject and to encourage one another. Two thousand people attended this conference. Other conventions followed, spreading the message of faith healing across the United States and Europe.

Before Boardman's work at Bethshan, Charles Spurgeon, famous pastor of the Metropolitan Tabernacle in London, was

---

[17] Chappell, *Great Things He Hath Done*, 126.
[18] Chappell, 136.

involved in healing work. According to Chappell, although Spurgeon did not focus on this topic in his sermons, he prayed for the sick regularly in his services. It was common for his church members to request prayer for healing, and many reported being healed.

Andrew Murray, a South African, received physical healing at Bethshan. He was a well-known evangelical of international repute who was influenced by both William Boardman and Otto Stockmayer. Murray accepted the doctrine of divine healing initially from the work of Dr. Cullis. He was a highly respected pastor of the Dutch Reformed Church and moderator of the South African Dutch Reformed Church who was considered the founding leader of the Keswick movement in his country. His books were read worldwide in multiple languages. Through his travels around the world, the messages of holiness and divine healing spread across the globe. David Duplessis, called Mr. Pentecost within the Pentecostal/charismatic movement, considered Murray his spiritual father. Murray came to believe that by accepting Jesus by faith as healer and physician and by exercising one's faith and will to begin acting as if one is healed, even when the symptoms are still visible, one can be healed. Through his associations with D. L. Moody and R. A. Torrey, he became a strong influence for divine healing in the United States.

A. J. Gordon, founder of Gordon College, became a key leader in the divine healing and Keswick movements.[19] He was the pastor of the prestigious Clarendon Street Church in

---

[19] Chappell, 143.

Boston and was a leader of the Keswick Holiness movement. His church was involved in many healing and relief efforts in Boston. Gordon also reached out to the Jewish and Chinese communities in the United States. The Boston Missionary Training School, the institution Gordon founded in 1889, later became the historic Gordon College. Graduates of this school went as missionaries to Africa, China, and India, and domestically to the American Indian territories in Oklahoma. Gordon served as a trustee of Dr. Cullis's faith work in Boston and supported Cullis's efforts to provide health care, education, social services, and spiritual care to the poor and needy in his community.

Gordon was influenced by D. L. Moody's ministry and was impacted by the instantaneous healings he witnessed through the prayers of believers.[20] His study of the Scripture concerning healing convinced him that Christ's earthly ministry was characterized by two major emphases: forgiveness of sin and healing of sickness. Gordon believed Matthew 8:17 taught that physical healing was provided in the atonement because Christ carried both our sin and our sickness. He frequently referred to Psalm 103:3 and pointed out that the promise of healing was unconditional. Since the Scripture taught that the prayer of faith shall save the sick and the Lord shall raise him up, he believed that it is inconsistent to confine divine healing to the apostolic age. He suspected that relegating the age of miracles to the past was the evidence of the modern church's impotence.

---

[20] Chappell, 144.

A. B. Simpson, founder of the International Christian and Missionary Alliance, was another great leader of the divine healing movement of the nineteenth and twentieth centuries.[21] Simpson held Friday healing services in New York City that drew thousands of people seeking healing prayer. While serving as pastor of the prestigious Thirteenth Street Presbyterian Church in New York City, he had received a healing at an annual faith convention held by Charles Cullis in Maine. He returned to New York City, resigned his church, and began a new work to reach the unchurched people of the city. His ministry established several branch churches, reaching out to different ethnic groups in New York City, and established rescue missions and many rehabilitation centers. He launched a powerful missionary program by founding a missionary training college, which later became Nyack College and Nyack Theological Seminary in New York.

Simpson's work became a denomination known today as the Christian and Missionary Alliance (CMA). The core doctrines of CMA were: Christ is Savior, Christ is sanctifier, Christ is healer, and Christ is the coming King. Simpson established a ten-day convention focusing on complete holiness and divine healing. At these gatherings, he hosted speakers such as R. A. Torrey, A. J. Gordon, Otto Stockmayer, Andrew Murray, and Carrie Judd Montgomery. Simpson asserted that divine healing is part of the complete redemptive work of Jesus Christ. He believed that sickness is the result of the fall, and divine healing is a benefit from the atoning sacrifice of Jesus.

---

[21] Chappell, 162.

Healing is a redemption right, purchased by the blood of Jesus Christ. Believers can commit their bodies to Christ and simply claim their promise of healing by faith. He also emphasized that believers need to act on their faith after the prayer of faith, claiming that Christ has already begun the healing. He advised the sick to ignore the symptoms of illnesses and go forward believing in the reality of their healing. Simpson was not against the use of medicine but was not a proponent of physicians and medical care. Although he did not strictly prohibit the use of physicians and medicine, he taught that any human attempt at helping the sick would imply a doubt of the reality of the healing.[22] He persuaded a great number of individuals to enter full-time ministry, with divine healing as a major emphasis of the ministry.

Women in Healing Ministry

Carrie Judd Montgomery was another impactful propagator of the divine healing message. As a person with roots in the nineteenth-century Holiness and healing movements, Montgomery became a bridge between the divine healing and Pentecostal movements as she became a part of the newly developing Pentecostal movement.[23] She was the first woman evangelist to travel as a healing evangelist. Montgomery established the first faith healing home on the American West Coast, claiming that her inspiration to do so was the work of Dr. Cullis. Having been healed of a

---

[22] Chappell, 177.
[23] Wayne E. Warner, "Montgomery, Carrie Judd" in Burgess, *NIDPCM*, 904–6.

severe disability under the ministry of Elizabeth Mix, she became associated with A. B. Simpson and the Christian Missionary Alliance and, though she had an Episcopal background, served as the first recording secretary of CMA and later as its vice president.

Montgomery insisted that we must simply believe because we are healed by the Word of God, based on Psalm 107:20. To receive divine healing, one must believe God's Word despite feelings or circumstances. God's promised blessing of healing is received by "acting faith," not "feeling faith." Montgomery believed that as believers praised and worshiped God, their feelings would naturally align with God's truth. Montgomery, with her husband, George Montgomery, moved to California in 1890 and founded a rescue and healing mission in San Francisco and established a faith home called the "Home of Peace" near Oakland. She went on to establish an orphanage and a Bible training college and started a Monday afternoon faith healing service in downtown Oakland.

In 1906, George Montgomery visited holiness preacher William Seymour's service at Azusa Street Mission in Los Angeles. Two years later, Carrie Montgomery received the baptism of the Holy Spirit and spoke in tongues at a friend's house in Chicago and became a member of the emerging Pentecostal movement. As a member of the Assemblies of God, she attended the first World Pentecostal Conference, held in London. On her return trip from England, she visited A. B. Simpson in Nyack and shared her Pentecostal experience. Simpson never subscribed to the doctrine of tongues but allowed Montgomery, considered a moderate Pentecostal, to share her Pentecostal experience with his congregation in Nyack. Montgomery's faith home continued to operate even after her death in 1946.[24]

Another well-known woman known for her divine healing ministry was Maria Woodworth-Etter.[25] A member of the United Brethren Church who joined the Church of God in Indiana later, she conducted preaching and ministry tours with great success. Some of her meetings brought together up to twenty-five thousand people in a single service. Attendees witnessed multitudes of people being healed, prophecies given, and manifestations such as singing in the Spirit, speaking in tongues, and dancing in the Spirit. Etter insisted that the power given to the apostles had never been taken back from the church and preached a strong message of divine healing. She was arrested on various occasions for "practicing medicine without a license." She traveled with an eight-thousand-seat tent and preached to the masses. She had a profound influence on Carrie Judd, whom she met in Oakland in 1889.

Aimee Semple McPherson was another female healing evangelist whom Etter influenced.[26] McPherson preached occasionally at Etter's Tabernacle in Indianapolis, and both became prominent personalities in the newly emerging Pentecostal movement. Etter conducted a five-month campaign for evangelist F. F. Bosworth in Dallas, and many of the early Pentecostal leaders attended her meetings. She became

---

[24] Chappell, *Great Things He Hath Done*, 162.
[25] Chappell, 161.
[26] C. M. Robeck Jr., "McPherson, Aimee Semple" in Burgess, *NIDPCM*, 856–59.

a strong link between the divine healing movement and the Pentecostal movement.

The Holiness Cradle

The Holiness movement became the cradle for the development of the divine healing movement in the second half of the nineteenth century. Holiness preachers spread across the nation the doctrine of entire sanctification, which included the doctrine of divine healing. At that point the doctrine of divine healing had become a major part of the Holiness credo. The debate on the issue of whether healing was in the atonement continued, and even those who did not theologically accept healing as an equal provision with salvation supported the ministry of the church based on James 5:14–16. Divine healing became a prominent teaching and a common practice in the Holiness movement. Donald Dayton concluded, "Pietism may have been one of the most important forces in the rise of the doctrine of divine healing."[27] In 1901, the general Holiness assembly declared formally that the sick are healed through the prayer of faith. It was article 5 of the six-point statement of faith.

The beginning of the twentieth century saw the rapid expansion of Holiness congregations in the South, Southwest, and Midwest of the United States. These churches and groups emphasized the ministry of healing. Some of them radicalized the doctrine and maintained that any use of doctors or medicines represented a lack of faith in Christ. Others cautioned believers

---

[27] Donald Dayton, *Theological Roots of Pentecostalism* (Grand Rapids: Baker Academic, 1987), 119.

not to abandon the divine healing doctrine because of fanatics. The two largest Holiness denominations that were eventually formed out of these churches—the Church of the Nazarene and the Pilgrim Holiness Church—embraced divine healing and incorporated the doctrine in their statements of faith.

Multiple Holiness groups and denominations merged to form larger bodies during this period. Some of these groups later became part of the Pentecostal movement. Some of the Holiness groups tended to be less radical in their views regarding the use of medicine. For others, salvation and healing were of the same theological importance, and those who consulted doctors were people of weak faith.

Dowie and Zion

John Alexander Dowie represented the radical group. He was called "the apostle of healing" of his day. Dowie formed the Divine Healing Association, which created a worldwide network of ministers and followers and founded the Christian Catholic Church. Dowie also established the largest divine healing home in the world in Chicago. He built an eight-thousand-seat tabernacle and filled it every Sunday.[28] Dowie insisted that supernatural healing always occurred instantaneously, and he vigorously opposed the use of physicians and medicines. One of his sermons was titled "Doctors, Drugs and Devils or the Force of Christ the Healer."[29] As far as he was concerned, A. J. Gordon, Maria Woodworth-Etter, and even R. A. Torrey and A. B. Simpson were heretics because they were not radical

---

[28] Chappell, *Great Things He Hath Done*, 185.
[29] Chappell, "Heal, Healing," 540.

enough for him. He insisted, based on Matthew 8:16–17, that Jesus healed all who were sick. He believed that disease is the devil's work, and it can never be God's will. Satan produces sin and disease, he taught, but Christ has delivered mankind from the power of the enemy. Dowie refused to pray for the healing of unbelievers, as he insisted that one must accept salvation first and pursue holiness. Holiness causes health.

Chappell detailed his work in Chicago. Arriving from Australia, Dowie began his work in San Francisco. Later he moved to the Chicago area, where his ministry produced several high-profile healings. Amanda Hicks, a cousin of President Abraham Lincoln, was one of the individuals healed under Dowie's ministry. As his fame increased, people traveled across the nation to be prayed for by him. Many were healed, and they left behind their crutches, braces, canes, and other prosthetics, and Dowie displayed them for the world to see. He received three thousand letters per week asking for prayer. In 1896, he bought the seven-story Imperial Hotel in Chicago and converted it into a faith healing home. He was granted personal audiences with two presidents of the United States—McKinley and Roosevelt.

Modeling the work of Dr. Cullis, Dowie reached out to the disinherited in society and offered them physical, spiritual, and economic assistance. His followers distributed food and clothing and helped people by cooking meals for them, scrubbing their floors, and assisting them in finding employment. Dowie fought against discrimination, racism, anti-Semitism, and other social evils. He purchased 6,500 acres of land north of Chicago and built the City of Zion as a self-supporting utopian community that was to be a model of a godly society. Zion grew to ten thousand residents in 1905, but due to a stroke he suffered and charges of financial mismanagement, he could not continue his leadership of Zion or his church. In any case, according to Chappell, Dowie reached more people worldwide with the message of divine healing than any other individual.[30] He became a model for healing evangelists of the twentieth century.

Dowie never became a Pentecostal, but his ministry in Chicago became a strategic center for the emerging Pentecostal movement, as it became the site where divine healing was added to speaking in tongues as a distinctive and vital doctrine of the Pentecostal movement. We will examine that connection in the next chapter.

---

[30] Chappell, *Great Things He Hath Done,* 217.

CHAPTER 7

DIVINE HEALING AND THE PENTECOSTAL MOVEMENT

The history of the Pentecostal movement in the United States begins in Topeka, Kansas, where Charles Parham led a Bible school.[1] In 1901, one of his students, Agnes Ozman, was filled with the Spirit and spoke in other tongues. A study of the book of Acts concerning the work of the Holy Spirit had led to this event. Parham began a Bible school in Houston, Texas, in 1905. William Seymour, a black Holiness pastor, attended his classes. Sadly, Seymour had to listen to Parham's teaching "from a hallway," as Parham "allegedly [seated] his white students in the classroom."[2] Nonetheless, Seymour embraced the Pentecostal message and in February 1906 went to Los Angeles in response to an invitation from a church there. Rejected by the group that had invited him due to his faith in

---

[1] R. Goff Jr., "Parham, Charles Fox" in Burgess, *NIDPCM*, 955–57.
[2] C. M. Robeck Jr., "William Joseph Seymour," in Burgess, *NIDPCM*, 1055.

speaking in tongues, Seymour started a new work on a small scale. Eventually, he found himself at the center of a global revival at a mission house on Azusa Street in Los Angeles.[3] The Pentecostal message of baptism in the Holy Spirit with the evidence of speaking in tongues went across the world through men and women who were impacted by the revival at the Azusa Street Mission. (There were concurrent moves of the Holy Spirit in other parts of the world, like Multi Mission in India, not directly related to Azusa.[4])

Charles Parham and Zion

Charles Parham was a Methodist pastor. He was a preacher of divine healing and a part of the divine healing movement before the revival with speaking in tongues at Topeka.[5] Parham had attended the meetings conducted by Holiness evangelist Benjamin Hardin Irvin and witnessed certain spiritual manifestations that Irvin called "the baptism of the Holy Spirit and fire." Parham was not receptive to what he saw at that point but kept wondering about the ways God reveals His presence among His people. He led his students in an investigation of this topic based on the book of Acts. During the last weeks of 1900, he asked them to find the common factor behind the birth of the church in Acts. The students identified tongues as

---

[3] Ruth Oberg, "Lessons from Azusa's Pastor: What Church Leaders Can Learn from William J. Seymour," in George P. Wood, ed., *Influence: The Shape of Leadership* (Springfield, MO: General Council of the Assemblies of God, 2022), 34.

[4] Saju Mathew, *Kerala Penthekosthu Charithram: The History of Pentecost in Kerala*, 2nd Malayalam ed. (Kottayam, Kerala, India: Good News, 2007), 31.

[5] Chappell, *Great Things He Hath Done*, 220.

that factor or evidence. Accepting the events in Acts as normative for their day, the students sought the same experience, and Agnes Ozman spoke in tongues. Parham and some of Ozman's classmates had the same experience a short time later.

Before his own Pentecostal experience at Bethel Bible School in Topeka, Parham was a proponent of the divine healing message. He had received a healing in 1897 and had started a ministry of preaching divine healing and praying for the sick.[6] He started the Bethel Healing Home in Topeka in 1898 which offered lodging and faith training for individuals seeking divine cure.[7] People came to his divine healing home from all parts of the nation, and many miracles were reported. To learn more about the healing ministry, Parham visited John Dowie's healing home in Chicago, Simpson's work in New York, and A. J. Gordon's ministry in Boston. After his experience of the baptism of the Holy Spirit, Parham emphasized his teaching on the baptism of the Holy Spirit with the evidence of speaking in tongues and seemed to have neglected the ministry of healing. He encountered much resistance to the new Pentecostal message, but Parham noticed that where people accepted the teaching of divine healing, they were more open to receive his new doctrine of tongues.

In 1906, Parham made a stop at Zion on a trip to Azusa during a time when Zion was amid a leadership struggle caused by Dowie's declining health. Parham was well received, but his new message of baptism in the Holy Spirit with the

---

[6] Chappell, 220.
[7] Goff, "Parham, Charles Fox," 955–57.

evidence of speaking in tongues divided the holiness people at Zion. There were strong dissentions, and Parham failed to become the leader of Zion.[8] But the Pentecostal group at Zion gained theological strength, and it produced many great leaders who carried the teaching of both divine healing and the baptism of the Holy Spirit across the United States and the world. It may be accurate to say that Zion was only second to Azusa in terms of the propagation of the Pentecostal message, merging the cardinal doctrines of the baptism in the Holy Spirit with speaking in tongues and divine healing. Although these doctrines were connected in Topeka, Zion became the crucible of the merging of these major theological ideas that became the most propelling message of the emerging Pentecostal movement at the dawn of the twentieth century.[9]

Healing Ministers from Zion

Paul Chappell traced the history of Zion City and Parham's Pentecostal pilgrimage there.[10] According to Chappell, Parham had great influence on the Christian Catholic Church (founded by Dowie) throughout North America. He was able to convert most of the churches belonging to this denomination to the Pentecostal doctrine. Some of his followers in the Christian Catholic Church became missionaries to several nations, including Australia, Holland, South Africa, and India. A number of prominent healing evangelists came out of Zion. One of the most well-known ministers among them was Fred F. Bosworth,

---

[8] Goff, 956.
[9] Chappell, *Great Things He Hath Done*, 224.
[10] Chappell, 222–29.

who held large gatherings in major auditoriums across America and Canada. He started a megachurch in Dallas, Texas, and became a pioneer of radio evangelism. One of his coworkers was William Branham, who became a recognized healing evangelist.[11] Bosworth's book *Christ the Healer* was widely read.

Another product of Zion was John G. Lake, who founded the largest Pentecostal work in South Africa, the Apostolic Faith Church. He also founded many churches on the West Coast of the United States.

Gordon Lindsay, the founder of Christ for the Nations in Dallas, was a Pentecostal healing minister who was born in Zion. He edited the influential *Voice of Healing* magazine, which brought together many healing evangelists and influenced the Pentecostal world with articles and reports about healing.[12]

Many churches and ministries across the United States were birthed by people who had been impacted by the Pentecostal revival at Zion led by Parham. Several founding leaders of the Assemblies of God denomination came out of Zion. The founder of the historic Stone Church of Chicago, William Piper, was a product of Zion. Piper opened a healing home. David A. Reed, a convert of Parham, oversaw this healing home. Later he worked with Aimee Semple McPherson, who founded the Pentecostal Foursquare Gospel denomination.

---

[11] David E. Harrell Jr., *All Things Are Possible: The Healing and Charismatic Revivals in America* (Bloomington: Indiana University Press, 1975), 10–52. Harrell gave considerable attention to pioneer Pentecostal healing ministers. He called Branham and Oral Roberts two giants of the movement.

[12] D. D. Bundy, "Lindsay, Gordon and Freda Theresa," in Burgess, *NIDPCM*, 842.

What John Alexander Dowie was to the Holiness divine healing movement, Charles Parham was to the Pentecostal movement. Parham's work inseparably linked divine healing and the baptism of the Holy Spirit with the evidence of speaking in tongues as two quintessential doctrinal pillars of the Pentecostal movement. Through his work through Dowie's Zion and the Catholic Christian Church and through the work of his disciple William Seymour at Azusa, Parham became a unique agent of the merging of the vital Pentecostal doctrines and their global impact. According to Paul Chappell, out of Azusa came the Pentecostal denominations, and from Zion City came the many independent churches and ministries that became a major segment of the modern Pentecostal movement.[13]

Sanctification, Healing, and the Baptism in the Holy Spirit

To understand how divine healing became a vital doctrine for the Pentecostals, one has to look at the evolution of three important theological concepts: salvation, sanctification, and baptism in the Holy Spirit. Historically these terms were understood differently, especially the baptism in the Holy Spirit. The Roman Catholic Church teaches that salvation, sanctification, and baptism in the Holy Spirit all happen at the same time when one is baptized in water. Water baptism is efficacious for salvation. Orthodox and Anglican churches also hold a similar view.

---

[13] Chappell, *Great Things He Hath Done*, 225.

The Reformation established that salvation is by faith alone. Water baptism is only the outward expression of an inward experience. Salvation and baptism in the Holy Spirit are simultaneous experiences. One receives the fullness of the Holy Spirit rather than being baptized in the Holy Spirit. When one is saved, one receives the fullness of the Trinity—Father, Son, and Holy Spirit. Sanctification begins at salvation, and it is progressive in nature. The Reformed view is held by Baptists, Presbyterians, Congregationalists, and the Disciples of Christ.

Within the Wesleyan Holiness tradition, one is saved by faith first and later would experience sanctification, which is a second spiritual blessing. Sanctification enables a believer to live a holy life. Sanctification is also called "pure love," "perfection," and "the baptism of the Holy Spirit." Methodists, Wesleyans, Nazarenes, and the Christian Missionary Alliance adhere to this position.

An emphasis on the baptism of the Holy Spirit took place within the Wesleyan Holiness movement, but without necessarily linking it to speaking in tongues. Divine healing was already a normative doctrine within this movement. Divine healing was a benefit of sanctification. Because sanctification was instant, healing of the body could also take place instantly.

The Pentecostals of the twentieth century found their roots in two Holiness camps: the Wesleyan Holiness tradition and the Keswick Higher Life movement.[14] The Wesleyan Holiness position held two separate works of grace: justification and

---

[14] R. V. Pierard, "Holiness Movement, American," in Walter A. Elwell, ed., *Evangelical Dictionary of Theology*, 2nd ed. (Grand Rapids: Baker Academic, 2001), 564–65.

sanctification. Justification happens at the time of conversion, and sanctification is a distinct second blessing. Sanctification is also known as Christian perfection, perfect love, and the baptism in the Holy Spirit. And those who reach Christian perfection no longer sin because the sin nature is eradicated, and they live a life of separation from the world. The Pentecostals who had their roots in the Wesleyan Holiness movement preached salvation, sanctification, and a subsequent experience called the baptism in the Holy Spirit with the evidence of speaking in tongues.

The Pentecostal group that developed out of the Keswick Higher Life tradition did not accept the doctrine of entire sanctification embraced by those in the Wesleyan Holiness movement. This group believed that sanctification is a progressive experience that begins at conversion. The moment of conversion is also the beginning of the sanctifying process, and the converted is empowered by the Holy Spirit to live a holy life. This empowerment of the Holy Spirit, which happens subsequent to conversion, is called the baptism in the Holy Spirit.

The Keswick Pentecostals do not believe that the sin nature is fully eradicated. They believe that the Holy Spirit enables one to live a pure life. The Higher Life Holiness movement embraced the gifts of the Holy Spirit, but without the requirement of speaking in tongues as initial physical evidence. The Wesleyan Holiness adherents also rejected the Pentecostal baptism in the Holy Spirit. So, there are two groups of tongues-speaking Pentecostals today: the Wesleyan Holiness Pentecostals, who believe in complete sanctification;

and the Keswick Holiness Pentecostals, who hold the position of progressive sanctification. Both groups embraced divine healing and speaking in tongues; one group presenting a three-step position, and the latter a two-step position, calling themselves the "finished work" group.[15]

Historian David E. Harrell summarized this transition: "The holiness movement of the late nineteenth century stressed personal holiness, or 'entire sanctification,' as evidence of the indwelling of the Holy Spirit. Pentecostals took this emphasis a step further in what some called a 'third work of grace,' while others omitted sanctification and considered 'baptism in the Spirit' the only subsequent experience to conversion."[16]

Pioneer Pentecostal Healing Ministers

As the Pentecostal movement grew and spread in the first four decades of the twentieth century, it encountered many threats and oppositions. The American fundamentalists condemned Pentecostalism as fanatical, and the Holiness adherents who did not accept the doctrine of the baptism of the Holy Spirit with speaking in tongues resisted the Pentecostal tongues.[17] However, the message spread far and wide. Among the global leaders of the movement were F. F. Bosworth of the United States and Smith Wigglesworth of England.

Canadian by birth, with her background in the Salvation Army, Aimee Semple McPherson became a prominent

---

[15] V. Synan, "Pentecostalism," in Walter A. Elwell, ed., *Evangelical Dictionary of Theology*, 2nd ed. (Grand Rapids, MI: Baker Academic, 2001), 901.

[16] Harrell, *All Things Are Possible*, 11.

[17] Pierard, "Holiness Movement," 565.

Pentecostal healing evangelist during the 1920s and '30s. She was married to a missionary who died in China. After returning to America, she began to preach across the country. She became well-known as the first female radio preacher who owned her own radio station. She built one of the largest churches at that time—the five-thousand-seat Angelus Temple in Los Angeles. At one point she conducted about twenty-one services every week. McPherson founded the LIFE Bible College and established the International Church of the Foursquare Gospel.[18] The name of the denomination stood for the four doctrinal pillars: Jesus Christ is Savior; Jesus Christ is healer; Jesus Christ is baptizer; and Jesus Christ is coming King.

A Methodist pastor, Dr. Charles S. Price experienced the baptism of the Holy Spirit through the ministry of McPherson.[19] A native of England who was trained in law, Price was so impacted by his new experience that he became an evangelist and reached many non-Pentecostals with the message of divine healing and the baptism of the Holy Spirit. Through his magazine, *Golden Grain*, and his healing ministry, he brought the message of divine healing to a great number of people.

By the end of Price's ministry, another notable person had entered the healing revival movement. William Branham conducted widely reported healing campaigns, which propelled the growth of the Pentecostal movement. Branham, a Baptist minister with limited education, experienced an encounter with an angel in which he was promised the gift of healing.[20]

---

18 Robeck, "McPherson, Aimee Semple," 857.
19 R. M. Riss, "Price, Charles Sydney," in Burgess, *NIDPCM*, 997.
20 D. J. Wilson, "Branham, William Marrion," in Burgess, 440–41.

Following this experience, he was called to pray for a pastor's dying daughter in St. Louis, Missouri. She was healed and fully recovered. This incident made him so well-known that some of his meetings were attended by twenty-five thousand people. His ministry drew other capable individuals who extended his influence and spread the message of divine healing. The famous Pentecostal evangelist Fred F. Bosworth joined his team, which expanded Branham's fame. Branham became the first evangelist to hold healing campaigns across Europe.

In 1951, Branham prayed for William Upshaw, a US congressman, and he was healed of a debilitating disease.[21] This brought national attention to his ministry and the message of divine healing. Branham influenced a great number of ministers to enter the healing ministry who, through their work, spread the word of healing within and beyond the Pentecostal movement.

Tommy Lee "T. L." Osborn was another missionary evangelist who was best known for his miracle ministry. With his wife, Daisy Washburn Osborn, as his associate minister, he established a ministry in Tulsa, Oklahoma, in 1949. Together they preached a message of healing and deliverance in over ninety nations for more than half a century. Hundreds of thousands of people attended some of their meetings. I was privileged to know T. L. Osborn personally.

Another person who had a great impact across the world through his healing ministry was Oral Roberts, founder of Oral Roberts University in Tulsa, Oklahoma, where I served

---

21 Harrell, *All Things Are Possible*, 35.

for nearly four decades. In terms of influence, as Billy Graham was to the saving of the soul in the twentieth century, Oral Roberts was to the healing of the soul and body. We will examine his life and contributions to spreading the teaching and practice of divine healing in the next chapter.

The Charismatic Movement

The 1960s saw the birth of the charismatic movement. The healing revival, which reached beyond Pentecostalism, was instrumental in the birth and growth of this movement.

One of the earliest individuals known for the ministry of healing within the charismatic movement was Kathryn Kuhlman. Her ministry focused on the mainline denominational churches. Oral Roberts considered her the greatest evangelist of the ministry of miracle power.

The global Pentecostal/charismatic movement claims more than 600 million adherents and is the fastest-growing religious movement in world history.[22] Considered the second wave of the Pentecostal movement, the charismatic movement has various groups within its embrace. The first group is comprised of people in the non-Pentecostal mainline denominations who believe in healing and the baptism of the Holy Spirit. (They accept any of the gifts of the Holy Spirit, not just tongues, as evidence of the baptism in the Holy Spirit and called tongues the "prayer language," a term Oral Roberts coined to reduce the stigma attached to Pentecostal tongues at that time.) These

---

[22] Todd M. Johnson, "Pentecostal/Charismatic Christianity," Gordon Conwell Theological Seminary blog, May 27, 2020, https://www.gordonconwell.edu/blog/pentecostal-charismatic-christianity/.

charismatics accept the doctrine and practice of divine healing but stay within their respective traditions. Started within the Catholic Church, this wave reached all major denominations. Francis MacNutt, a Harvard graduate and former Catholic priest, through his writing and healing ministry, was a major influencer within the Catholic Church.[23] A similar movement has been active in the Episcopal Church.

Other mainline denominations followed, some with people who had experienced the baptism in the Holy Spirit even before 1960, which is considered the birth year of the charismatic movement. Harald Bredesen, a Lutheran minister, was one of them. He was baptized in the Holy Spirit in 1946. Tommy Tyson, a Methodist pastor who became the first chaplain at Oral Roberts University, was another leader. Tyson received the baptism in the Holy Spirit in 1951. James Brown, a Presbyterian minister, received the baptism in the Holy Spirit in 1956.[24]

Demos Shekarian, a businessman and founder of the Full Gospel Business Men's Fellowship International (FGBMFI), was influential in spreading the word about healing and the Holy Spirit across the nation and around the world.[25] Shekarian was a part of the advance group that prepared for Roberts's crusades on some occasions, and Roberts helped make Shekarian's dream of creating a marketplace spiritual movement come true. His organization was instrumental in bringing the Pentecostal message outside the Pentecostal denominations by

---

[23] Harrell, *All Things Are Possible*, 228.
[24] P. D. Hocken, "Charismatic Movement," in Burgess, *NIDPCM*, 477–81.
[25] Harrell, *All Things Are Possible*, 146–49.

holding its meetings in religiously neutral places, like hotels, and targeting primarily the marketplace.

A crucial event in terms of the initial explosion of the charismatic movement was the experience of Dennis Bennett, an Episcopalian pastor in Van Nuys, California.[26] He was baptized in the Holy Spirit and was instrumental in several others having the experience. On April 3, 1960, he shared his experience with his congregation and announced his resignation from the pastorate. This was followed by a pastoral letter from the bishop of Los Angeles forbidding speaking in tongues. The story was carried by both *Time* magazine and *Newsweek* and brought it to the attention of the entire nation. This was the beginning of the great charismatic awakening outside the Pentecostal circles.

As mentioned earlier, the charismatics accepted speaking in tongues as the evidence of the baptism of the Holy Spirit, like the Pentecostals, but they merged their experience with their respective traditions. By embracing the empowerment of the Holy Spirit rather than sanctification like the Holiness brethren, the charismatic movement democratized the ministry of healing and deliverance. Individuals sat in chairs at breakfast and lunch meetings in hotels and restaurants as others laid hands on them and prayed, and scores of people of all backgrounds were filled with the Holy Spirit, many testifying of receiving healing and miracles. FGBMFI's *Voice* magazine propagated the news across the globe and FGBMFI chapters mushroomed in many nations.

---

[26] Harrell, 227.

Another group within the charismatic movement is the word of faith movement. The late Kenneth Hagin Sr. is considered the father of this segment.[27] Hagin had a global impact in spreading the word of healing through his books, media programs, and the school he established in Broken Arrow, Oklahoma. The Rhema Bible Training Center has trained thousands of students from all over the world. Prominent leaders among the healing evangelists who were impacted by Hagin include Kenneth Copeland, Fred Price, Benny Hinn, and Rodney Howard-Browne. Hagin taught a radical form of divine healing. His followers, especially the earlier ones, believed that accepting medicine is a sign of lack of faith. Additionally, he added concepts such as positive confession and denial of symptoms to the Pentecostal doctrine of divine healing. It has been pointed out that his teachings were influenced by the controversial teachings of pastor and author E. W. Kenyon, but he denied the charge.

Another group within the charismatic movement is the third wave, which includes those in the mainstream evangelical churches who embrace signs and wonders as the current work of the Holy Spirit but choose not to be identified as Pentecostals. Some consider this group a fourth wave. This group sees signs and wonders and healing in relation to church growth as articulated by Peter Wagner, who was a professor at Fuller Theological Seminary. John Wimber was a major figure in this group.[28] The Vineyard Fellowship churches Wimber led belong

---

27 R. M. Riss, "Hagin, Kenneth E.," in Burgess, *NIDPCM*, 687.
28 C. P. Wagner, "Wimber, John," in Burgess, 1200.

to the third wave. Wagner and Wimber taught a course called "Signs and Wonders" at Fuller Theological Seminary, and it launched a great controversy among traditional evangelicals. While the Fuller controversy was going on in the 1980s, the Oral Roberts University Graduate School of Theology and Missions promoted itself as "the Signs and Wonders Seminary" under then-dean Larry Lea.

It may be appropriate to say there is another group within the charismatic movement that consists of thousands of independent churches, including many megachurches, across the world. They promote charismatic worship, divine healing, and the expectation of signs and wonders. There have been attempts to organize a formal network of these churches, but they were never successful. The formation of the International Charismatic Bible Ministries (ICBM) by Oral Roberts, despite several ICBM conferences held on ORU's campus, was such an effort. The ICBM did have some success but failed to create a lasting organization.

Oral Roberts University has been at the crossroads of all the Pentecostal waves of the past. Through the recently developed Empowered21 network, with which I was involved as the dean of the ORU College of Theology and Ministry, Dr. William M. Wilson, fourth president of ORU, has attempted to bring members of all three-plus waves under an umbrella called the Spirit-empowered movement. This network, formed after the centennial of the Azusa Street revival, is still a work in progress. All waves of the Pentecostal movement, despite their theological orientations and varying traditions, believe in the teaching and practice of divine healing.

CHAPTER 8

ORAL ROBERTS AND HEALING EVANGELISM

Oral Roberts was born in small-town Bebe, Oklahoma, in 1918 as the fifth child and youngest son of a Pentecostal Holiness pastor.[1] Diagnosed with tuberculosis at age seventeen, Roberts was healed miraculously through prayer. A clinic in Ada, Oklahoma, confirmed the healing. On the way to the prayer meeting where the healing had taken place, young

---

[1] As a chaplain at the former City of Faith Hospital and professor and dean at Oral Roberts University, I have presented my personal experiences with the Oral Roberts Ministries as well as studies of Oral Roberts's theology of healing at various venues in the United States and other nations. Academic versions of this information have been published in theological journals, including *Spiritus: ORU Journal of Theology* (vol. 3, no. 2, article 13, available at https://digitalshowcase.oru.edu/spiritus/vol3/iss2/13). This chapter and the following two chapters are indebted to my presentations and published papers in general, and particularly to the *Theological Journal of Hunsei University* which granted permission to use/adapt the material. Please see details in footnote 1 of chapter 10.

Roberts had heard God's voice saying that he would be healed to take God's healing message to his generation. As if to confirm the voice he had heard, God healed Roberts's stuttering also.

These healings had a great impact on his outlook on sickness and health. He preached his first sermon two months after his healing, then followed his father's footsteps in 1936 and became an ordained Pentecostal Holiness (PH) minister.

Roberts married Evelyn Lutman, a schoolteacher, in 1938, and he pastored four churches between 1941 and 1947. He received theological education at two institutions: Oklahoma Baptist University and Phillips University, which later became Phillips Theological Seminary. During those years, he and Evelyn had four children.

Roberts was not a happy local pastor, as he tried to do his very best for his church and denomination, sacrificing much and putting his young family through many hardships. His denomination honored traditional pastors who conformed, but conformance was not a strength for him.

Roberts believed in healing, and as a Christian minister, he wanted to give sick people opportunities to experience healing. His vision for healing was not limited to members of his congregation or denomination alone, and his definition of health was not limited to the physical body. He sought a wider healing ministry.

In 1947, Roberts left the local pastorate and started an independent healing ministry. He launched a healing crusade that year and published his understanding of healing in a book titled *If You Need Healing, Do These Things*. He was willing to let go of the local pastorate permanently and continue the crusade model of evangelistic healing ministry if it could financially support itself. The first crusade, held in Enid, Oklahoma, paid for itself, and that was his sign to continue. A failed attempt to kill him by a strange man at a crusade, where a bullet flew just inches above his head, unexpectedly gave Roberts and his ministry instant fame.

Roberts traveled across the country, conducting healing crusades in large tents. These tent meetings of the 1950s were well-known. The size and impact of the crusades kept increasing. Eventually, the tents became traveling cathedrals, the last one seating 12,500 but attracting as many as 15,000 people. The monthly magazine *Healing Waters,* which later was renamed *Abundant Life*, helped spread Roberts's message of healing. Radio networks carried his ministry and message across the country and beyond. Several crusades were held outside the United States. Over the years, more than three hundred crusades were held, and according to close associates, Roberts personally laid hands on and prayed for an estimated two million people.

By the 1950s, television was becoming a household necessity, and it was rapidly changing American culture. Roberts saw this new invention as an opportunity to bring his crusades to the living rooms of America. He pioneered televangelism. Through television, millions of people belonging to various Christian traditions and many unchurched witnessed the miracles of healing taking place in his crusade tents. They sought his prayer and sent money to support his ministry. By the 1970s, 64 million people were watching Roberts's programs through 525 TV stations, and by the 1980s, he was receiving five million letters per year, many containing financial gifts.

Oral Roberts became a household name, and Oral Roberts Ministry became a formidable spiritual force in America. Roberts's growing ministry of healing evangelism embodied a unique theology, one rooted in Pentecostal Holiness tradition but enhanced by Roberts's personal experiences and the expansion of Pentecostalism into the mainline denominations. This theology and its wider influence were also enhanced by the founding and resources of organizations such as the Full Gospel Business Men's Fellowship. At the heart of this theology was healing, later articulated as whole-person healing, wrapped up in a pneumatology that Roberts taught as "Holy Spirit in the Now!"

While his television program remained the number one syndicated religious program in America for three decades, Roberts was busy writing books about his life, ministry, and theology. The focus of his writing remained on healing, the Holy Spirit, and the principles of seed faith. Due to the nature of his ministry, most of Roberts's writing was aimed at nonacademic audiences, and many academic readers miss the complexity of his theological thinking. Roberts was a well-read person who had an appreciation for the life of the mind. His major theological tenets, especially about healing and wholeness, are well thought-out. Some of his theological positions were historically developmental in nature.

The foundation of Roberts's healing theology is a simple biblical concept: God is a good God (Ps 107:1), and He wants to heal the sick. (Roberts was quick to add that the devil is a bad devil.) The nation in the 1950s seemed unprepared for such an affirmation about God. Roberts believed it and declared it across the world, but people who looked for theological nuances were frustrated. Misunderstanding, persecution, or rejection, even by his own denomination, did not stop Roberts from declaring it. He had found an audience elsewhere that was responding very positively to his message. Roberts added these ideas to his concept of God:

1. You will be in a great position to have health and success if your relationship with God your source is right.
2. Your life will be completely different if you learn to plant good seeds with God and with people you like or dislike.
3. You can expect many miracles for yourself if you have a right relationship with yourself and with God.[2]

His first book presented six steps of healing:

1. Know that it is God's will to heal you and make you a whole person.
2. Remember that healing begins in the inner man.
3. Use a point of contact for the release of your faith.
4. Release your faith.
5. Close the case for victory.
6. Join yourself to companions of faith.[3]

In Roberts's thinking, releasing one's faith is the central issue in healing, and there is a key to opening up this process. He called it the *point of contact.* This is the way Roberts explained it:

---

[2] Oral Roberts, *Better Health and Miracle Living* (Tulsa, OK: Oral Roberts Evangelistic Association, 1976), 11–23.
[3] Roberts, 11–19.

Your point of contact can be one of several things. Mine is my right hand. Though there is no healing virtue in my right hand, God spoke to me and told me that I would feel His power through my right hand. It is a sensation of God's presence. When I lay my hand on the head of the person seeking God's healing and begin to pray, I often feel this power going through my right hand. The moment I feel it, my faith is very strong. This point of contact helps me to release my faith to God. Also, it helps the person seeking healing. When my faith and his faith contact with God, the healing begins. This is the point of contact we have used in our crusades, either through my hands or those of our team members. However, there are many other ways—such as the anointing oil of James 5:14, 15, the laying on of hands in Mark 16:17, 18 and the blessed cloths of Acts 19:11, 12. What does it matter what the point of contact is if it helps you release your faith?[4]

Later on, he defined the point of contact in three steps related to the concept of seed faith: (1) Make God your source (Phil 4:19); (2) Give and it shall be given to you (Luke 6:38); and (3) Expect a miracle (Mark 11:24).[5]

For those needing very practical steps to follow a healing path, Roberts supplied a list of seven "rules of healing":

---

[4] Oral Roberts, *If You Need Healing, Do These Things* (1947; Tulsa, OK: Oral Roberts Ministries, 2002), 47.
[5] Oral Roberts, *Miracles of Healing for You Today* (Tulsa, OK: Oral Roberts Ministries, 1982), 166.

1. Recognize that sickness is the oppression of the devil and that God wants you to be well and happy.
2. Believe the message of deliverance, no matter who is God's messenger.
3. Go where the power of God is, even though you may have to change your attitude and way of life.
4. Put your faith in God, not man. Remember, the man of God is the instrument. God is the healer.
5. Accept God's correction, for He knows best.
6. Lose yourself, for then you can become a new person.
7. Use a point of contact and be healed, a whole person again.[6]

Roberts's teaching on seed faith and miracles is incorporated into his theology of healing. The result is a nine-step prescription:

1. Get God into your life in a way He has never been there before.
2. Get your attitude in the direction of living instead of dying.
3. Put your attitude into action. DO SOMETHING. Make some decisions and get going.
4. Plant. Take your life—your money, your time, your love, your good attitude—and invest it in God's fertile soil.
5. Make your seed-planting a point of contact for each point of need in your life.
6. Grab hold of each burst of healing you receive.

---

[6] Roberts, *If You Need Healing, Do These Things*, 48.

7. Place the name of JESUS above the name of anything that causes you to have disease.

8. Run toward the goal of whole health that God has for you.

9. Decide today that you are going to carry out this prescription.[7]

Healing is related to faith, and faith comes by the hearing of the Word of God. Therefore, preaching of the Word is central to Roberts's teaching on healing. To him, healing faith is directly related to the hearing of the Word of God.

Oral Roberts was a healing evangelist, and he was seen as a man who believed in miracles. He was a man of faith who earnestly prayed for healing. He had a strong faith-based healing theology that was not simplistic. As a master communicator, Roberts did not believe that a half-hour TV program was the place to cover all the theological nuances. However, he did not hesitate to give the full version of his theology in his teachings on the campus of Oral Roberts University and in his books. Many still do not know that Roberts was not a "traditional" Pentecostal faith healer who rejected medicine as a natural means of healing. He was open to both natural and supernatural ways of healing. In fact, Roberts did not separate the natural from the supernatural. To him, he was dealing with a continuum, allowing easy movement from the natural to the supernatural and vice versa: "Both natural and supernatural healing powers work together for the healing of people, thus demonstrating that ALL HEALING IS DIVINE. . . . So we

---

[7] Roberts, *Miracles of Healing for You Today,* 163–64.

have Jesus healing not only by faith but also by putting within that sphere of healing the physician, which means from our Lord's standpoint, ALL HEALING IS DIVINE whether it's medical or by prayer and faith."[8] Roberts advised his followers to value the instrument of healing but worship the source—God.[9]

Classical Pentecostals and some charismatics who initially revolted against Roberts's position on medical treatment eventually found it generally acceptable. Many old-time Pentecostals experienced real relief from condemnation poured out on them by their faith communities for reaching out to the medical profession for help.

Roberts was not afraid to address the issue of unanswered prayer. He also addressed death and dying in the healing ministry.

"It is appointed unto men once to die, after this the judgment" (Hebrews 9:27). Death is a divine appointment. Death is classed as an enemy, our final enemy. But even in the process of dying I have seen miraculous things happen—release from pain, even the disappearance of the disease. You may ask, how then could the person die? Because there is a time to die, as well as a time to be born (Ecclesiastes 3:2). Sick or well, you are going to die. Sickness unchecked can hasten it. However, when death's time comes nothing will hold it back. We must be prepared to go at any moment (right in our heart with God and people).[10]

---

[8]   Roberts, *Better Health and Miracle Living*, 182.
[9]   Roberts, 187.
[10] Roberts, 188.

Roberts's theology of death was biblical. He was a realist and a healer at the same time. In *Better Health and Miracle Living*, he captured a conversation he had with a physician regarding patients who die after prayer for healing is offered. He compared his healing work as an evangelist to that of a physician who tries hard to heal the patients but is not successful always. He said:

> There have been times I have prayed for persons I felt would recover; some did and some did not. But I know that I am not God, only His instrument. My part is to pray, His is to make the final judgment. I pray for healing because I believe it is God's purpose to make people well. However, I don't always know when a person is going to die, or shall we say, is going to meet his divine appointment—so I pray with all the faith I have just as you, as a physician, use all your skill to make the person well.[11]

On other occasions he said that God heals in three different ways: instantly, gradually, and ultimately in the resurrection. This was not something commonly heard among charismatic healing ministers.

Roberts's healing theology was rooted in the atonement and what he called the "covenant right." He believed that from the front of the cross we see forgiveness and from the backside we see "the full measure of God's desire to heal us." At the cross, Jesus received upon Himself our sins and, with

---

[11] Roberts, 262–63.

them, all our diseases. All our sins and diseases were absorbed by Jesus into Himself. Roberts's commentary on the Bible says, "Our sins HAVE BEEN forgiven. Our diseases WERE HEALED. The victory has been won by Jesus and by our FAITH we can receive of God's redemption, the full measure of our deliverance."[12]

The sick must claim their covenant right. They must contend for their covenant right of healing. This is in the context of a spiritual battle between Satan's oppressive forces and God's power that is ready to release healing. Roberts connected this concept of battle with the idea of a point of contact. He commented on the healing of Jairus's daughter, for instance: "You are in between. Jairus held onto his point of contact, and it worked to keep his faith operating. When you ask God to heal you, if you are serious, there will be a tremendous conflict. But if you continue to look to God, your source of healing, He will give you the courage you need. . . . He had SAID, 'Lay your hands on her and she will be healed.' SAYING it started his point of contact."[13] The healing process involves believing, fighting one's fears, not doubting, and saying words of faith as a point of contact.

A point of contact makes faith "a definite act of believing." The woman with the issue of blood touching Christ's garment was using a point of contact. She was not just "finger touching," Roberts added. "She was touching Him with her FAITH. . . . Faith for healing is a definite transaction. It springs loose

---

[12] Oral Roberts, *Holy Bible with Personal Commentary by Oral Roberts* (Tulsa: Oral Roberts Evangelistic Association, 1981), 64.
[13] Roberts, 28.

what God has already made available for you and me in the covenant. HE HAS ALREADY DONE IT."[14]

Roberts sought biblical insights regarding unanswered prayers. He tried to understand God's no in light of His love and goodness. He concluded that God's no is not necessarily no. It means He has a better way. God's refusal is subject to change when we conform to His will. He wants what is ultimately best for us. God had a better way for Paul. His thorn became an instrument to keep him humble and dependent on God. "When God says wait, it means that in a special way His will or purpose is involved . . . When Jesus told Mary and Martha to wait, His will was to perform a greater miracle that so many more would believe on Him."[15]

This is why R. A. N. Kydd called Roberts's theology of healing "quintessentially Pentecostal." He noticed that Roberts's healing theology oscillates between two poles: "The first pole in Roberts' healing theology is certainty. Some Pentecostals have held this position without qualification, but Roberts did not. As with most Pentecostals, there is another pole in Roberts' teaching on healing—sovereignty. Roberts did not embrace either pole, but rather oscillated between them."[16] Many among Roberts's followers, however, did not hear his commitment to God's sovereignty. They heard a "more sure word" (see 2 Pet 1:19).

Roberts was not just a man of faith; he was also a man of hope. He expressed his theology of hope in his well-known

---

[14] Roberts, 27–28.
[15] Roberts, *If You Need Healing, Do These Things*, 30–33.
[16] R. A. N. Kydd, "Healing in the Christian Church," in Burgess, *NIDPCM*, 710–11; Mathew, "Oral Roberts' Theology of Healing," 7.

slogans, which he popularized over the years: "Expect a miracle" and "Something good is going to happen to you!" It is fair to say that his healing theology was rooted in a charismatic theology of hope. This theology goes beyond possibility to expectation.

In 1965, Roberts started Oral Roberts University (ORU) with three hundred students. It was formally dedicated in 1967, with Rev. Billy Graham giving the inaugural address.

ORU was born out of the fires of healing evangelism and built on Oral Roberts's theology of healing and wholeness. By the time the university was established, Roberts's theology was fully developed as a doctrine of whole-person healing and living. The university was his way of perpetuating this theology through whole-person education, that is, education for the total of a person: body, mind, and spirit. Thus, ORU was a pioneer in promoting the whole-person philosophy of education. Even today, physical exercise and spiritual disciplines are required of all students at ORU. Thousands of ORU graduates are serving God and humanity across the world.

In 1978, Roberts founded the ORU School of Medicine. This and his City of Faith Medical and Research Center (COF) were bold initiatives built on Roberts's confidence in what he had learned and practiced about healing. The COF, a part of the ORU School of Medicine, opened on the ORU campus in 1981 as an effort to implement the concept of whole-person medicine. The massive sixty-story building with two million square feet of floor space was dedicated to offering medical treatment through healing teams consisting of physicians, nurses, chaplains (called prayer partners), and other professionals. We will examine the story of the City of Faith, built at great expense, to merge medicine and prayer in the next chapter.

Roberts served as the president of ORU from 1965 to 1993. His son Richard L. Roberts became president of the university in 1993 but eventually had to resign due to financial and governance challenges. Following two interim presidents, Dr. Mark Rutland became the third president of ORU on July 1, 2009, followed by Dr. William M. Wilson in 2013.

Roberts impacted many spheres. He brought forth a paradigm shift in global evangelism by introducing healing evangelism through tent meetings and the media. He pioneered the concepts of whole-person education and whole-person medicine. He is considered the father of the charismatic movement, and it was he who developed the unique theological concepts of "seed faith" and "point of contact" in relation to the healing ministry.

Oral Roberts was loved and respected by Christians all over the world. At times he was a controversial figure, but even his critics respected his integrity and good testimony. Along with Rev. Billy Graham, he was known as one of the top two great religious leaders of twentieth-century America.

Oral and Evelyn Roberts lived an exemplary married life for sixty-six years until her death in 2005, having lost two of their children before her death. They had twelve grandchildren and many great-grandchildren.

Roberts died on December 15, 2009, in Newport Beach, California. I have not met anyone like Oral Roberts, and I doubt I ever will again. He was a one-of-a-kind gift to this world.

CHAPTER 9

CITY OF FAITH: AN EXPERIMENT IN MERGING MEDICINE AND PRAYER

This chapter on the City of Faith (COF) Hospital is written from my perspective as a former COF chaplain and "healing team" member and draws on former COF physician Roger L. Youmans's *Healing Team Concepts Manual,* a class reader printed by the Oral Roberts University Bookstore for fourth-year medical students at the former ORU School of Medicine. Youmans and I were co-teachers of the course titled "Healing Team Concepts." I am also indebted to conversations with several former COF leaders and a presentation made by pioneer ORU medical school professor Dr. John Crouch at the COF in fall 2015. Let us begin the chapter with why the COF was founded.

The Problem with Modern Medicine

Despite its great advancements, modern medical practice has a problem: it is designed to treat the patient's symptoms rather than the patient. Modern medicine does very well in terms of addressing the needs of the body, but its techniques normally deal with only one dimension of the person. Once a problem is diagnosed using all the resources of modern technology, physicians make very advanced assessments and treat the problems for the purpose of eliminating the symptoms. Other dimensions of the problem are referred to specialists, such as psychiatrists. Although psychiatry is supposed to deal with the mind and emotions, modern psychiatry mostly depends on drugs and chemicals to try to reduce the symptoms rather than deal with the real issues involved. Normally, doctors treating the body and psychiatrists and other professionals dealing with the mind do not deal with the spiritual aspects of the person. Of course, in many places there are chaplains to whom these issues are referred, but often they or local clergy are not intentionally and significantly integrated into the treatment teams or plans. This has been a concern for some for a long time.

Tournier's Challenge

Paul Tournier, a Swiss physician, was much interested in medicine and Christianity. In his pioneering work, *The Healing of Persons*, Tournier called attention to the deeper aspects of a person's sickness and symptoms. He pointed out that a person was more than the combination of the various aspects of his or her life. Tournier established an annual medical gathering in Switzerland to discuss the concept of the whole person and was able to influence thousands of doctors from all over the world to practice medicine with a whole-person perspective.

Tournier taught the importance of listening to the patient and the multiple issues and relationships in the patient's life that have an impact on his or her sickness and symptoms. He felt that people's relationship to God must be a factor in the overall medical treatment. Tournier's model required more time per patient on the part of physicians, raising the cost of treatment, which turned out to be a demotivator. In any case, by pointing out the need for doctors to share their humanity with patients by combining compassion and expertise, Tournier made a significant contribution to his profession.

Paul Tournier was a Christian but the medical practice he recommended was not explicitly Christian. An American surgeon, William S. Reed, took up Tournier's method with an explicitly Christian emphasis. He instructed doctors to pray with their patients and to be involved with them in a subjective way. Reed advised doctors to get involved with their patients' spirituality. Through his book *Healing the Whole Man* and through his annual physician conferences, Reed influenced many in his profession. He advised doctors to pay attention to spiritual, psychological, and somatic diseases. Most of the doctors who took Reed's instructions found that the model required more time and produced less income.

Five Spiritual Laws

Loring T. Swaim, MD, a noted orthopedic surgeon and a Harvard professor, published the results of his research on patients with arthritis in the book *Arthritis, Medicine and the Spiritual Laws* in 1962. He was a traditional medical practitioner following normal protocols but noticed certain emotional/

spiritual issues related to his patients who suffered from rheumatoid arthritis. He observed that disturbing emotional experiences had a bearing on the onset and recurrence of disease. By studying these factors from his Christian perspective, Dr. Swaim came up with five spiritual laws of health that could help his patients promote healing and prevent recurrence.

Dr. Swaim noticed that the most common emotions that had manifested preceding attacks of arthritis were severe hurt and bitterness. He also noticed that in almost all cases there was some remembrance or reliving of the negative emotions before a subsequent recurrence. Hurts, bitterness, and self-pity were seen in a predictive way in these patients. So Swaim developed what he called the five spiritual laws to offer to patients. They include the following:

1. the law of love, Matthew 22:39, John 15:12
2. the law of apology, Matthew 5:23–24
3. the law of change, Matthew 7:5
4. the law concerning fault-finding, Matthew 7:1
5. the law of forgiveness, Matthew 6:14

These spiritual laws were based on the words of Jesus as recorded in the Gospels. They have an impact on people's emotional well-being, and according to Dr. Swaim, even to their physical condition. Dr. Swaim did not stop practicing standard medicine. Like his contemporaries, he applied standard treatments for his patients, but his observations helped patients apply the spiritual principles to their lives and thus enhanced their healing. He believed that his approach treated the patients as whole persons.

The Adventists

Taking the patient as a whole person and considering the emotional and spiritual aspects of the person, even when the presenting problems are only physical, is critical. However, due to personal preferences and financial stresses, physicians do not often practice whole-person medicine. It is easier to treat the symptoms and send the patient home. In terms of promoting the importance of dealing with a patient's body, mind, and spirit to minister healing in the practice of medicine, the history of the Seventh-day Adventists is significant. Ellen White, a cofounder of the Adventists, began teaching and writing about health and well-being in 1864, shortly after the founding of the organization. She taught the following principles and required the new organization to put them into practice as well:[1]

1. The importance of diet and foods and the need to follow a balanced diet.

2. The importance of pure drinking water, fresh air, sunlight, exercise, rest, and abstinence from tobacco and other harmful substances.

3. The idea that the body is the temple of God and following these health principles would prevent the onset of sickness.

4. The health of the mind is as important as the health of the body. Mental health is an important aspect of a person's well-being.

---

[1] See "Fundamental Beliefs of Seventh-day Adventists," ASTR (Office of Archives Statistics, and Research), accessed August 23, 2022, https://www.adventistarchives.org/sdafundamentalbeliefs, and Ellen White, *Good Health* (1880–1889), https://egwwritings.org/book/b440.

5. Spiritual health is vital to well-being. One must develop Christian character and engage in Christian service.
6. The importance of hygiene for health and wellness. All laws of nature are designed for our good. Hygiene is a very important matter for health maintenance.

White not only taught and spread her thinking through her writings, but she also established several educational facilities to promote her ideas. In addition to many schools and colleges, her organization established the famous Loma Linda College of Medicine.[2] Incorporated in 1905, it was initially purposed as a college of medical evangelists, and today it is considered a world-class school of medicine. The Adventists operate hundreds of hospitals all over the world. They are known for their abstinence from smoking and drinking and for their concern for good diet and other health habits. Despite doctrinal differences with this group, one must pay attention to the healthy lifestyle they propose.

The Field of Medicine in the 1970s

By the 1980s, some studies had demonstrated that a wholistic approach to medicine can have greater impact and even economic advantage due to the speed of recovery, the reduced number of hospital days, and so on, but their impact on the actual practice of medicine was insignificant. Some non-Christian models of wholistic medicine were also emerging, but they were more syncretic and highly influenced

---

[2] See the history of the institution at "History," Loma Linda University, accessed August 23, 2022, https://home.llu.edu/about-llu/history.

by non-Christian religions. Often called holistic medicine, these models did not evidence the ethical concerns and spiritual priorities of a Christian approach.

This was the general background of the medical establishment in America when the City of Faith Medical and Research Center was built on the campus of Oral Roberts University in Tulsa, Oklahoma, according to Oral Roberts, to merge medicine and prayer. Whole-person medical practice from a strictly Christian perspective involving an intentional team approach remained mostly in theory in the 1970s when Roberts decided to launch the City of Faith Medical and Research Center. The City of Faith was a uniquely Christian whole-person healing effort.

There was another pressing need Roberts was trying to address at that time. There were many who were not thrilled about seeing Oral Roberts, a "faith healer," as the founder of a medical school that was accredited by the American Medical Association, and the local hospitals were against having another competing hospital in Tulsa. Initially, only one hospital provided opportunities for students of the ORU medical school for practical training. Roberts was under pressure to find or create sufficient clinical settings for these students. So out of the necessity to have a place to train students and to return to the healing roots of his ministry with an explicit whole-person approach, he established the City of Faith Medical and Research Center. The massive City of Faith complex had three towers: a sixty-story clinic, a thirty-story hospital, and a twenty-story research center. The institution was built with user-friendly floor plans and the latest available technology, and it opened on November 1,

1981. The founding of the ORU medical school and the City of Faith Medical and Research Center (COF) were bold moves. They were also the visible evidence of Oral Roberts's faith in God, as he had to raise hundreds of millions of dollars for the debt-free construction of the complex from his very ordinary "partners" who each donated $77 per square foot.

Healing Teams

Healing teams of doctors, nurses, ministers, and other professionals functioned with full institutional support at the City of Faith. A sixty-foot-tall healing hands sculpture made of bronze (similar to the familiar praying hands) at the entrance of the towers (now moved to the entrance of the university) symbolized the merging of prayer and medicine, the natural and the supernatural. To Roberts, one of these hands represented the apostle Paul's hand (minister) and the other, Luke the physician's hand. Despite local controversies related to Oklahoma politics and the sheer resistance against a faith-healer evangelist being involved in academic medical education, the initiative to merge medicine and prayer was watched by the whole nation and caught the attention of Christians everywhere.

Along with highly skilled medical professionals, the City of Faith had clinically trained professional chaplains called prayer partners, and licensed counselors. The chaplains were supported by hundreds of trained lay prayer partners from Tulsa-area churches. Students from the ORU seminary joined the staff to learn and to practice healing ministry in an institutional context. The City of Faith had an approved Clinical

Pastoral Education program led by a former president of the College of Chaplains (now Association of Professional Chaplains), Herbert Hillebrand. The entire Spiritual Care Division, which included two departments—Pastoral Care and Counseling—was led by a retired army chaplain, Col. Duie Jernigan, PhD. I joined the staff of the COF Hospital two weeks before it opened and later became the leader of the Pastoral Care Department of the Spiritual Care Division, following David D. Dunning, who was a US Navy chaplain before joining the City of Faith staff.

Luke (a physician) and Paul (a minister) were working together at City of Faith, Roberts told the world, and patients came from all over the world to receive healing and miracles through the work of healing teams. They wanted to receive healing through medicine and prayer. Oral and Richard Roberts and other members of the Roberts family joined the chaplains from time to time to pray for the sick. I accompanied them on many occasions as they prayed for the patients.

The City of Faith was a dynamic place of medicine, prayer, and healing. It was also a place of pain, suffering, and death, like any other hospital, but many patients and their families did not expect these at a place of faith and prayer and found it hard to accept. Doctors were trying to learn to share professional power and work with other team members. Medical students were being trained to value teams and to pray for the sick. Nursing and theology students were also enrolled in training programs. Territorial disputes between departments and professions were common. The demand for healing and miracles from the patients, based on their understanding of the mission of the institution and the perceived promises made by Roberts on his television programs, made work very challenging for all concerned.

Prayer was a part of everything that happened at the City of Faith. Patients were prayed for at all important areas within the clinic and the hospital. Admissions staff prayed for patients at the entry points. Doctors and nurses prayed. Prayer partners prayed day and night. The social workers and pharmacists prayed as patients were discharged. Healing testimonials abounded. Speedy healings, unexplainable recoveries, and plain miracles were happening, but pain, suffering, and death were also present, sometimes much more than expected because the hopeless patients rejected by other medical facilities often came to the COF as a last resort.

Lack of healing and miracles was very upsetting to many patients and families, especially those who had alienated their local doctors and caregivers by rejecting their prognoses and traveling to Tulsa. When the miracles did not happen, they were in serious trouble with their hometown doctors. The lack of miracles upset many staff members too, some of whom had given up very good positions at well-known hospitals to join the COF experiment.

Ministry Between Miracles: A Model of Pastoral Healing

Although clinical pastoral care was being offered by well-trained professionals, no one was articulating a model of pastoral care that could accommodate both miracles and death. Charismatics generally did not have a strong theology of death at that time. Some patients from the word of faith movement were dying without saying goodbye to their families because they believed that doing so expressed a lack of faith. There were patients "confessing" and "claiming" supernatural reversal of completed body-altering surgeries, encouraged by well-known "healing ministries." They wanted the staff chaplains to join their confessions!

Chaplains were meeting and reflecting on their ministry experiences. Professional development sessions dealt with issues that were unique to the City of Faith. Medical professionals were looking to spiritual care staff for support and prayers and for a theological frame of reference to deal with the issues of life and death the COF uniquely brought out, all in spite of many speedy healings and miraculous recoveries.

A five-step model of pastoral care was being practiced. Dr. Stan Beason, a United Methodist pastor trained in clinical pastoral education (CPE) was training lay prayer partners on the five steps. These steps included *incarnational presence, listening, information gathering, prayer,* and *referral.* Dealing with questions of theodicy (lack of answer to prayer, suffering, etc.) was left to the professional prayer partners, who received the referrals from the lay prayer partners.

Chaplains who were trained at traditional seminaries and typical CPE programs were unsure about handling the lack of miracles of healing in a context that seemingly promised them. A model of pastoral care congruent with the theology and dynamics of the organization was badly needed. The goals of traditional pastoral care—healing, guiding, sustaining, and reconciling—had to be adjusted for "healing" to include the supernatural and the natural and "sustaining" to include dealing with extreme suffering and disappointments.[3]

Pastoral care has not been a major thrust of the modern Pentecostal movement from its beginning. Due to the eschatological evangelism to which the Pentecostal movement was deeply committed, the need for pastoral care was not given priority. The Pentecostals' commitment to charismatic worship and puritanical holiness also encouraged this neglect.[4] Although the Pentecostal denominations were beginning to support clinical training and chaplaincy, especially military chaplaincy, they were under attack by missionary evangelists and pastors, such as Jimmy Swaggart, who preached that Pentecostals were "backsliding" to counseling.

I was trained in pastoral care at Yale Divinity School and had completed advanced CPE at Norwich Hospital in Norwich, Connecticut. Miracles were not a part of the vocabulary of my teachers or the trainers I had. But I was a third-generation Pentecostal who believed in miracles of healing. Traditional pastoral care did not speak about miracles much. On the other hand, charismatics who believed in miracles did not have much room for traditional pastoral care. Oral Roberts did not even like the term *chaplain* because of some unsatisfactory experiences he had had at other hospitals. He saw chaplains as people who did not focus on the prayer of faith. That is why the City of Faith chaplains were called prayer partners.

---

[3] William A. Clebsch and Charles R. Jaekle, *Pastoral Care in Historical Perspective* (Englewood Cliffs, NJ: Prentice Hall, 1964), 8–10.

[4] Thomson K. Mathew, *Ministry Between Miracles: A Biblical Model of Spirit-led Pastoral Care* (Kottayam, Kerala, India: Goodnews Books, 2020), 25.

This was the context when, beginning with a sermon I preached based on John 6 in the medical school chapel, I was able to develop a Spirit-led model of pastoral care. Seeing pastoral care as a ministry between miracles, this theory provided a four-step pastoral care response: (1) enabling patients to *listen* to the voice of God, (2) helping them to *learn* the will of God, (3) assisting them to *live* fully human lives by faith while they await their healing, and (4) encouraging them to *be loyal* to Jesus Christ during the dark hours of their lives as they await a new chapter of life to begin with the possibility of healing and miracles.[5] The idea was that "Expect a miracle," "Something good is going to happen to you," and real healings could coexist at the City of Faith with pain, suffering, and death.

Great Outcomes, a Failed Experiment, World Impact

City of Faith provided ample evidence that whole-person medical care from a Christian perspective, where prayers of faith and spiritual interventions were given equal validity as traditional medical care, could produce natural and supernatural healing. Unfortunately, the City of Faith was closed due to financial and other reasons, and the experiment was discontinued. The planned research to study the distinctive impact of the new health-care model was never completed. But from personal experiences and hundreds of anecdotes from coworkers, I can confidently testify that God heals naturally and supernaturally and that whole-person health care is superior

---

[5] Details of this model are found in Mathew, 137–52.

to traditional medical practice. Divine healing and miracles are possible even in this scientific age. Responsible merging of medicine and prayer will never produce worse outcomes than what traditional medicine accomplishes alone.

Doctors, nurses, chaplains, and others involved in the City of Faith project were profoundly changed by the experience in life-transforming ways. Many professionals took the lessons and conclusions from the City of Faith to their future assignments and made significant contributions in their respective fields. Most prominent among these was the founding of the In His Image Family Practice Residency Program in Tulsa by Dr. John Crouch and colleagues,[6] which has produced hundreds of board-certified physicians who are involved in whole-person medical and healing work in the United States and many other nations. Dr. Mitch Duininck, Dr. Edward Rylander, and other leaders carry on this work today with significant world impact. My son-in-law, Dr. Fiju Koshy, is a product of this program. He has been involved in whole-person medical missions in Asia and Africa.

---

[6] Dr. John Crouch was chairman of the ORU School of Medicine Family Practice Department when the school closed. The founding of the In His Image Residency Program took visionary cooperation and considerable efforts by three of his colleagues: Dr. Pat Bolding, who had been a resident at ORU and was then a faculty member; Dr. Mitchell Duininck, who was an ORU medical school graduate who had done residency at ORU and was a faculty member; and Dr. Ed Rylander, who was also an ORU medical school graduate who had done residency at ORU and was a faculty member.

CHAPTER 10

DAVID YONGGI CHO: AN ASIAN VOICE OF HEALING

Davids Yonggi Cho was the founding pastor of the largest Christian congregation in the world, with over five hundred thousand members, located in Seoul, Korea.[1] Raised in a Buddhist home, Cho was converted to Christ, filled with

---

[1] This chapter is adapted with permission from a paper I presented at a conference held at Hansei University in Seoul, Korea, comparing the healing theologies of Oral Roberts and Paul Yonggi Cho, which was published bilingually. See *Theological Journal of Hansei University* (vol. 6). Please see references to the original paper: 톰슨 매튜 (Thomson K. Mathew), "오랄 로버츠 목사와 영산 조용기 목사의 치유신학에 대한 비교 평가," 『영산신학저널』 6, no. 2 (2006); 38–69 in Korean. This is the Korean version of the article, printed in the *Journal of Youngsan Theology* (영산신학저널), an academic journal published by the Institute/Hansei University Press of Hansei University. This paper was included in the first volume of books named *Dr. Yonggi Cho's Ministry & Theology*, which consists of two volumes. Thomson K. Mathew, "Oral Roberts and David Yonggi Cho: A Comparative Evaluation of Their Theologies of Healing," *Dr. Yonggi Cho's Ministry & Theology*, vol. 1 (Gunpo, Korea: Hansei University Logos, 2008): 285–343 in English.

the Holy Spirit, and called to the ministry. After graduating from the Assemblies of God Bible School, he started a tent church in the slum area of Seoul in 1958. He began his ministry among the poor and devastated people of postwar Korea. Challenging his cultural and religious context in many ways, Cho preached a theology of hope, healing, and blessing to build the largest local church in the world. In addition to his ecclesiastical positions, he served as president of Church Growth International, a globally influential organization. Cho has written numerous volumes on healing, the Holy Spirit, positive thinking, prayer, and church growth, much of which are available in English.[2]

A Personal Story

I had few opportunities to visit Rev. Yonggi Cho at his residence during my visits to Korea. When I was with Dr. Vinson Synan during one visit, we had a private dinner with Reverend Cho. He shared several stories with us during that dinner. Dr. Synan wanted to know his estimate of the state of the church in Korea. In response to the question, "How is the Assemblies of God doing in Korea?" Dr. Cho laughingly replied, "I am the Assemblies of God in Korea."

I heard another memorable story that night about the Pentecostal Holiness Church—Dr. Synan's denomination, where his father was bishop at one time—which denied young Yonggi Cho's application for ordination, stating that he lacked the qualities required to be a good pastor. Dr. Synan apologized

---

[2] D. J. Wilson, "Cho, David (Paul) Yonggi," in Burgess, *NIDPCM*, 521–22.

on behalf of his denomination and reminded Dr. Cho that it was not his first apology for the bad assessment.

Theology

David Yonggi Cho's theology is summarized in what he called the fivefold gospel and the threefold blessing. The fivefold message of the gospel, according to Cho, includes salvation; the baptism in the Holy Spirit, which he calls fullness of the Holy Spirit; divine healing; the second coming; and blessing. William Menzies acknowledged that four of the fivefold messages are borrowed from American evangelical Christianity, particularly the cardinal doctrines of the Assemblies of God.[3] His teaching on the blessing came from 3 John 2: "Beloved, I wish above all things that thou mayest prosper and be in health, even as thy soul prospereth" (KJV). The threefold blessing includes salvation, health, and prosperity.

Yonggi Cho believed in a concept called "the fourth dimension." He believed that we live in a three-dimensional world but there are spiritual realities beyond the third dimension. The fourth dimension is a spiritual realm.[4] There is also an evil spirit world beyond the third dimension that is controlled by Satan. "The evil spirit world, the kingdom of darkness, which is controlled by Satan, belongs to a spirit realm with supernatural power but it is not the spiritual realm. Totally different from the

---

[3] William W. Menzies, "David Yonggi Cho's Theology of the Fullness of the Spirit: A Pentecostal Perspective" in *David Yonggi Cho: A Close Look at His Theology and Ministry*, ed. Wonsuk Ma, (Philippines: APTS Press, 2004), 36.
[4] David Yonggi Cho, *The Fourth Dimension*, 3rd ed. (Seoul; Seoul Logos, 1979), 46.

realm of the Holy Spirit, counterfeits of healing and miracles can take place in the evil spirit realm, imitating the power of the work of God as the magicians of Egypt did."[5] Visions and dreams are the languages of the fourth dimension.[6] Word-based imagination, faith, and intense prayer are involved in tapping into the realm of the spirit.

The Source of Illness

To Yonggi Cho, the source of illness is Satan, and the cause of illness is sin. "When man turns away from God and sins against Him, he will receive his rightful wage, that of death (Romans 6:23). As such, Christ described the devil as the one who steals, kills, and destroys men (John 10:10). . . . In addition to the devil and our sins, illness originates from God's curse upon mankind. Although God is good, He is also righteous. Because of man's sin, the righteous God judges mankind for his sin."[7] Cho believed that when man turns away from God and goes against His Word, he is cursed by God and placed in a vulnerable position, subject to being robbed, killed, and destroyed by the devil. Another cause of illness is inappropriate dietary habits.[8] Additionally, following their own physical desires and goals, drinking alcohol, and smoking can also affect human beings negatively.[9] Fundamentally, according to Cho, whatever causes the illness of the soul can also become causes for man's physical ills.

---

[5] Cho, 46.
[6] Cho, 51.
[7] David Yonggi Cho, *How Can I Be Healed?* (Seoul: Seoul Logos, 1999), 29, 31.
[8] Cho, 34.
[9] Cho, 35.

The way to divine healing is claimed through Christ's redemption on the cross.[10] To enjoy the blessing of healing, one must first prepare the vessel in which blessings are to be received. Cho provided the following steps toward healing:[11]

1. We must have hope of perfect health.
2. We must confess and be forgiven of our sins.
3. We must forgive others, even our enemies.
4. We must have faith.
5. We must ask God to help us stay holy and free of sin.

According to Cho, those who do not wait in anticipation of God's divine intervention will not experience healing.[12] "When we have a burning desire and hope of healing, God will extend His blessing to us and free us from our illnesses."[13] Since sin is the basic source of illness, one must first get rid of sin.[14] "When we repent of the sins we have committed through our actions and thoughts and we change our thoughts to be in line with the righteousness of God, 'preventing Satan from entering and influencing us,' God will find it pleasing to heal us of our ills."[15] We also must forgive our enemies. Christians must learn to forgive others in the name of Jesus Christ. Once we are forgiven of our sins, we can be healed of the ills that arise from our guilty conscience.[16]

---

[10] Cho, 51.
[11] Cho, 52.
[12] Cho, 53.
[13] Cho, 55.
[14] Cho, 59.
[15] Cho, 60.
[16] Cho, 63.

Faith

Faith is the requirement for healing. One needs to have faith that God will indeed heal him or her. "When we pray with faith that God will heal us of our ills," said Cho, "God will indeed heal us."[17] Cho defines two categories of faith. One is called "general faith," that is, the type of faith that all human beings subscribe to as they live in this world. For example, people deposit money in the bank or fly on an airplane, actually, by faith. The second category of faith, according to Cho, is given by the Holy Spirit. This faith is discovered in the Bible. This type of faith is required to experience healings and miracles, which defy the laws of nature. "Without this faith, none can please God and none can receive divine healing."[18] The basis of healing is the cross of Jesus Christ. Cho sees faith for salvation and faith for healing as one and the same. "If it were true that divine healing was a time-limited phenomenon manifested only during the days of Christ and His disciples, then we must conclude that the miracle of salvation was also limited to such a time period."[19] Jesus endured severe suffering "to provide us with health."[20]

Cho called faith the energy of the Holy Spirit.[21] "Faith is also a certificate of title of things we hope for eagerly. . . . Although you may not see any evidence of it with your eyes

---

[17] Cho, 69.
[18] Cho, 71.
[19] Cho, 72.
[20] David Yonggi Cho, *Use Your Faith Energy* (Seoul: Seoul Logos, 2004), 59.
[21] Cho, 30.

or hear any sound with your ears, even as your future seems dark, when faith energy starts to work within you and makes you think, '[I]t's already come about,' then you become a person of faith."[22]

Practically speaking, Cho said we must draw a picture of ourselves as totally healed, on the authority of God's Word. We should confess our healing with our mouths, "because there is healing power in our speech. Since speech comes through thinking and faith in healing changes our thinking, our speech now commands the whole nervous system of the body so that it works to produce health. In accordance with that command, the energy of life is provided for life."[23]

Power of Words and Faith

Words and speaking were also important to Cho. Words have power. In fact, Cho believed that faith is the unity of belief and words.[24] For faith to become effective, one's words have to be consistent with one's faith. At the same time, just because one can speak eloquently about faith, it does not mean one possesses faith. Faith involves words and actions. "To speak creatively you must use the power of faith."[25] Based on Luke 5:20, "[Jesus] saw their faith," Cho believed that through

---

[22] Cho, 29.

[23] David Yonggi Cho, *Salvation, Health, and Prosperity, Our Threefold Blessings in Christ* (Altamonte Springs, FL: Creation House Strang Communications, 1987), 154.

[24] Cho, *Use Your Faith Energy*, 33.

[25] David Yonggi Cho, *Born to Be Blessed* (Seoul: Seoul Logos, 1993), 41.

one's actions, one's faith becomes visible.[26] Faith is based on
the Word of God rather than on our senses, and it requires
obedience and waiting.[27] Faith is also a kind of knowledge.
"It is not sense knowledge," but "revelational knowledge."
It cannot be obtained without the work of the Holy Spirit.
"Faith in God never comes to man except by the revelation
of the Holy Spirit."[28] Faith requires visions and dreams. It is
the invisible vessel holding one's dreams. These dreams are
birthed in one's heart through the Word of God. "Faith comes
by hearing, and hearing by the word of God," the book of
Romans reminds us (10:17).

More than anything else, faith is required for healing.
Mere intellectual understanding will not produce the kind
of faith required for healing. Prayer and fasting can increase
one's faith. Faith is not a vague hope for the future; it is always
a thing of the present.

Faith without hope is miserable. "No matter how much
turbulence and hardship there may be in your life you should
look up to the sky and believe in the promises of God and
His miracles," Cho wrote.[29] Those who exercise their faith in
hope and wait on God receive their healing.

Healing was a matter of great theological importance in
Cho's thinking. Not only is healing a direct part of the fivefold
message—salvation, the fullness of the Holy Spirit, divine
healing, blessings, and the second coming of Christ—it is

---

[26] Cho, *Use Your Faith Energy*, 37.
[27] Cho, 72–73.
[28] Cho, *Born to Be Blessed*, 13.
[29] Cho, *Use Your Faith Energy*, 107.

also a part of the threefold blessing—salvation, health, and prosperity. Healing is central to the gospel. It is normative in the kingdom of God. Healing is key to evangelization. Miracles and healing can facilitate the spreading of the gospel.[30]

Miracles cannot be explained by human logic. They are beyond human comprehension. But believers can expect miracles. "When we believe God, speak positively and pray until such confidence of answered prayer reaches us from God, we will see miracles operate in our lives."[31] Blessings follow those who qualify. The beatitudes summarize the qualifications necessary to receive blessings in this life and the life to come.[32]

Methods

Yonggi Cho discussed at length the various methods of healing, such as prayer and laying on of hands, touch or contact, spoken commands, and anointing with oil, in his books. As Jesus and His disciples used these methods, we may also do these things in the name of Jesus Christ. Prayer is a prerequisite for healing. "Christ himself prayed in private," Cho wrote, "although in public He healed others, taught them. . . . Therefore, we must prepare through prayer."[33] Cho recommended the following steps to prepare oneself to receive the blessing of healing:[34]

---

[30] Cho, *How Can I Be Healed?*, 101.
[31] Cho, *Born to Be Blessed*, 46.
[32] Cho, 61.
[33] Cho, *How Can I Be Healed?*, 84.
[34] Cho, *Salvation, Health, and Prosperity*, 144–55.

1. Eagerly desire health.
2. Repent of all sins.
3. Receive and give forgiveness.
4. Have faith.

According to Cho, our salvation not only changes our souls, but it changes our way of living from being a curse to being a blessing. Salvation also changes "our flesh from being subject to death and disease to being subject to life."[35] Cho believes that God's desire for all of His people is good health. He stated that the house called "Three-fold Blessings" has three rooms. The first room is the prosperity of the soul. The second room is where all things will go well with us. In the third room we find that it is God's will that we have good health.[36] Salvation provides us the right to healing because in salvation the three evils that brought sickness to us—the devil, sin, and the curse—are defeated. The devil provides the energy for the disease. When one confesses one's sins and believes in the precious blood and power of the Lord Jesus, one's sins are forgiven and he or she is delivered from the curse of the Law. We are also delivered from the torment of sin and sickness of the body: "for the moment when Jesus forgave the sins of the sick, the devil lost the basis on which he could keep them as servants in his bondage. The fact that we have been delivered from sickness attests to the other fact that we have been set free from the bondage of the devil."[37] The gift of divine healing

---

[35] Cho, 16.
[36] Cho, 115.
[37] Cho, 121.

is an authoritative gift appointed by God.[38] As evidence that we have been forgiven, God heals us.[39]

Cho connected the work of healing with the coming of the kingdom of God. Kingdom people have been healed from sickness of both spirit and body. They are called to live healthy and dynamic lives. Many are sick and feeble because the kingdom of heaven has not yet come upon their spirits and bodies. The preaching of the gospel produces the presence of the kingdom of God.

Cho's Pro-Medicine Stance

Cho disagreed with those who insist that to be healed by God, one must forsake modern medicine. "It is alright to be treated by a doctor and modern medicine," he said.[40] Based on Matthew 9:12, where Jesus said, "It is not the healthy who need a doctor, but the sick" (NIV), Cho believed that the Bible acknowledges the existence and function of doctors. He affirmed that God can and does heal through doctors and medicine, but he considered it foolish to depend only upon modern medicine. God is the source of all healing. "God can heal us directly through divine healing or He can heal us through doctors and modern medicine."[41]

Cho did not believe that the ministry of healing is limited only to those with the gifts of healing. Anyone who has faith can pray for the sick. The qualification for healing ministry in

---

[38] Cho, 135.
[39] Cho, 141.
[40] Cho, *How Can I Be Healed?*, 95.
[41] Cho, 96.

Mark 16:17–18, according to Cho, is faith. He believed that those who have the gifts of healing simply have greater power to minister healing. Cho advised against depending only on doctors because modern medicine does not have treatment for all illnesses, the cost of treatment is high, and there is a danger of misdiagnosis. As the causes of illnesses can be different, so must the treatment. If the cause is spiritual in nature, we must first repent. Then we can ask God for healing.[42] Cho found a relationship between the measure of faith one has and the healing one receives. We are healed according to the measure of our faith. Cho did not believe that shamans can bring about true healing. As "demons do not drive out other demons,"[43] those who claim that they have been healed through shamans are deceived. The devil cannot do anything beneficial for man and does not desire to see people live in health.

Prevention

Cho's teaching on healing included preventive measures. He believed that when stress and emotional distress are left untreated, they will cause physical pain and illness. He was aware of the environmental changes that are heaping great stress upon people today, causing depression, hypertension, and other diseases. He suggested several preventive measures to maintain health, including regular rest, stress reduction, and changing the environment. Taking a trip with a good friend and being introduced to new things and surroundings can refresh one's mind and body. Walking through the mountains and breathing

---

[42] Cho, 98.
[43] Cho, 99.

in fresh air can relax one's mind. Cho recommended regular physical exercise to reduce stress. He believed that God sent Elijah on a trip for forty days partially as a strategy to change his environment.[44] Although Elijah asked God to take his life (see 1 Kgs 19:1–9), God gave him rest instead. "God caused Elijah to fall into a deep sleep, waking him to feed him. With this repeated measure, Elijah returned to health and God made Elijah walk to Mount Horeb to hear God's message."[45] Cho believed that internal strength can withstand external pressure. The One who dwells in the believer is greater than the one who dwells in the world (1 John 4:4). "With such occupancy, there is no external pressure great enough to lead us to destruction."[46]

Cho gave the following prescription to maintain mental health: confess sin; learn to be content; get rid of jealousy, hatred, and anger; don't worry or be anxious; and always be filled with the Holy Spirit.[47] To maintain health after divine healing, he recommended these steps: maintain a close relationship with Jesus Christ, live a holy life, learn to give, and take good care of one's body.[48] Taking care of the body, to Cho, included a well-rounded diet and moderate exercise. The things that promote sickness include smoking, drinking, illicit drugs, a poor diet, and lack of sleep.[49]

---

[44] Cho, 118.
[45] Cho, 122.
[46] Cho, 123.
[47] Cho, 123–29.
[48] Cho, 130–35.
[49] Cho, 135.

In terms of health maintenance, Cho emphasized giving as providing for the poor. He taught that those who believe in God should take care of those who are poor and that when we show greater mercy and concern for the poor and offer them assistance, God will bless us. In fact, Cho believed that if we turn away from those who need our help or abuse and suppress them, we ourselves will become targets of illness (see Deut 28:22).[50]

Unanswered Prayers

Cho acknowledged that not all people who are ill receive God's divine healing. But he believed that the problem lies not with God, who is perfect, but with those whom God does not heal. They may be guilty of the sin of unrepentance. On the other hand, it may simply be God's time for a person to die, or perhaps God has a special plan for that individual.[51] In any case, sin blocks the blessings that are headed our way (see Jer 5:25). When sinners are healed, it is for the purpose of moving their hearts to accept Christ.

Cho also stated that sometimes it is not God's will for a person to be healed. The variables in this regard are (1) the will of God, (2) repentance of the one who is ill,[52] (3) lack of faith, and (4) lack of persistence in prayer. With regard to the time element in healing, he said, "God may answer within a short period, or He may answer after what seem ages to us, due to the devil getting in the way." Healing may not happen because

---

[50] Cho, 134.
[51] Cho, 135–40.
[52] Cho, 137.

God may have a different plan for the patient. For example, by allowing Satan to test Job's faith, God showed Satan that he was wrong.[53] (He also ended up blessing Job with twice as much as he had possessed before his sickness!) Paul's thorn in the flesh kept him from being proud.

Regarding the suffering of the innocent, Cho said, "At times, God does allow in His will even faithful Christians to be afflicted with illness."[54] When we see our Christian friends being afflicted with illness, we should not be too quick to judge them. Nor should we be too downtrodden when we are not made well from our own illnesses.[55] "It is not always easy to discern between the suffering brought by Satan that God would rather deliver, and the suffering that God would use to bring about the flow of redemptive grace. . . . Do not become discouraged or go from one famous evangelist to another to receive their words. But let God show you His will through your prayer, fasting and faith."[56]

Theological Themes
Common to Roberts and Cho

We have examined the teachings of two prominent ministers of healing. It is beneficial to see areas of agreement and disagreement between them. Roberts and Cho have acknowledged their mutual relationship and admiration for each other. Younghoon Lee, the senior pastor who replaced Rev. Yonggi

---

[53] Cho, 139.
[54] Cho, 139–40.
[55] Cho, 140.
[56] Cho, *The Fourth Dimension,* 3rd ed., 112.

Cho at Yoido Full Gospel Church, has written about their lifelong relationship.[57] Each has written introductions to the other's books.[58] Obviously, the senior minister, Roberts, had a tremendous influence on Cho. Menzies and Myung Soo Park believe that Cho's theology had the most influence from Roberts, especially on the threefold blessings. Cho himself stated, "I, personally, have received many challenges from Roberts, his emphasized message, 'Dear friend, I pray that you may enjoy good health and that all may go well with you, even as your soul is getting along well' (3 John 2) has become the testimony in my pastoral career. . . . I love Pastor Oral Roberts with all my heart. He has prayed for my personal career and life and kept encouraging me."[59]

Roberts and Cho shared the following common themes in their theologies of healing:

1. Health is not merely the absence of illness; it is the wholeness of being.

2. The human body, mind, and spirit are connected at very deep levels.

3. An individual has significant influence over his or her health and well-being. Personal spiritual disciplines, habits, and choices are related to one's wholeness or lack of health.

---

[57] Younghoon Lee, "Oral Roberts and David Yonggi Cho: A Life-Long Relationship in Theology and Ministry," *Spiritus* 4, no. 1, article 4 (2019).

[58] See, for example, Cho, *Salvation, Health, and Prosperity,* 7–9.

[59] David Yonggi Cho, *Church Growth: Do You Really Want It?* (1995), 19–20, quoted in Myung Soo Park, "David Yonggi Cho and International Pentecostal/ Charismatic Movements," 2002 *Young San International Theological Symposium* (Korea: Hansei University, 2002), 227.

4. Faith is the key to divine health and healing.

5. God is a good God, and He wants us to be whole.

6. God is the source of *all* healing. Whether healing results from medical intervention, prayer, natural healing processes, or a combination of these, all healing comes from God.

7. We can expect divine intervention in our lives. Although healing cannot be guaranteed for each person in every situation, God can be trusted to heal us naturally and supernaturally.

8. God determines the timing of healing. Sometimes healing comes instantaneously; at other times it comes more gradually.

9. Suffering and death are realities of life in this fallen world; the suffering of believers cannot always be explained.

10. Healing is normative in the kingdom of God.

11. Faith is required for healing.

12. Miracles of healing promote evangelization.

13. Believers can expect miracles of healing.

14. Faith for salvation is faith for healing.

15. Faith for healing involves believing, speaking, and acting.

16. The basis of divine healing is the atonement.

Theological Differences

Yonggi Cho's theology has been criticized for its syncretism with shamanism.[60] This criticism, leveled by major personalities

---

[60] Allen Anderson, "The Contextual Pentecostal Theology of David Yonngi Cho," in Wonsuk Ma, ed., *David Yonngi Cho: A Close Look at His Theology and Ministry* (Baguio, Philippines: APTS, 2004), 142.

such as Harvey Cox and Walter Hollenweger, has been challenged by Myung Soo Park and others.[61] Hollenweger and Cox reportedly have acknowledged the weaknesses of their criticisms. Cho discredited the effects of shamans' claims of healing and explained that any such healing is in fact demonic deception. He distanced himself from such and strongly advised his people to do so.

As we have seen, Roberts has been called the quintessential Pentecostal. His theology was rooted in classical Pentecostal doctrines. However, a more appropriate label for his theology might be Pentecostal/charismatic. Cho's theology would also fit in this category. Although the theologies of both Yonggi Cho and Oral Roberts can be classified as Pentecostal/charismatic, one can notice differences in emphasis, conceptualization, vocabulary, and articulation in their theologies of healing.

Cho was called to minister to a people who were devastated by occupation and war. Although Roberts was raised in a poor Pentecostal Holiness parsonage, his healing ministry thrived first of all in America, a prosperous nation. Some of the differences in emphases and in development might have to do with this contextual difference. The desperate needs of his people forced Cho to proclaim a theology of healing and blessings. His study of the Bible, pastoral reflection, and influence and modeling from Roberts resulted in Cho's theology. A desperate desire to break out of the poverty mentality of the post–world war Pentecostals persuaded Roberts to look deeply into the Gospels for a more dynamic and positive message of healing, well-being, and the power of the Holy Spirit.

---

[61] Menzies, "David Yonggi Cho's Theology of the Fullness of the Spirit," 27–42.

A Difference in Concept: Supernatural versus the Fourth Dimension

Roberts's "supernatural" and Cho's "fourth dimension" may not be the same conceptually. The fourth dimension is in the realm of the spirit. Cho found demonic and divine activity in this realm. He said that he reached this understanding as a revelation in response to his questions to God about why shamans claimed healing and miracles.[62] The fourth dimension contains the third dimension. It is something beyond the natural. Conceptually, it appears compartmentalized. "The first three dimensions are the boundaries which govern the material world," wrote Cho. "However, there is a greater dimension which governs and includes the lesser. That dimension is the realm of the spirit, the fourth dimension."[63] Cho saw visions and dreams as the instruments of the fourth dimension.[64] Roberts's supernatural, on the other hand, is not a compartment different from the natural or containing the natural; it represents a continuum. He wrote, "GOD DOES NOT SEPARATE THE NATURAL AND THE SUPERNATURAL IN YOUR LIFE. . . . God doesn't separate them. He never has. He doesn't today. He never will."[65] That is why Roberts could expect a miracle every day. To Cho, living in the fourth dimension meant living in the Spirit, and it seems to take one beyond the three-dimensional boundary.[66]

---

[62] David Yonggi Cho, *The Fourth Dimension*, vol. 2 (South Plainfield, NJ: Bridge Publishing, 1983), 36–37.

[63] Cho, 37.

[64] Cho, 50.

[65] Roberts, *Miracles of Healing for You Today*, 35 (see chap. 8, n. 5).

[66] Cho, *The Fourth Dimension*, vol. 2, 55.

Differences in Emphasis

a. Faith and a Point of Contact

Roberts taught that a point of contact will help one release his or her faith to God. The point of contact could be anything from anointing with oil to giving out of one's need—anything that releases one's faith. Cho referred to the point of contact, but the emphasis is not there. He encouraged fasting, prayer, all-night prayer, and so on to increase one's faith but did not necessarily refer to them as points of contact. Cho saw faith as energy.[67] It is connected to the word of God and one's own speech. To Roberts, faith comes by hearing the Word of God, which supplies and sustains hope and expectation. He did not promote fasting, all-night prayer, and so forth; instead, he emphasized the idea that God has given to each person a measure of faith. The important thing is not the amount of faith but the capacity to release the faith one has.

b. Visions, Dreams, and Imagination

Cho places a greater emphasis on the involvement of the mind in one's healing. Some have accused him of being a Christian Scientist. Park does not believe that is a fair criticism because Cho does accept the reality of symptoms and connects them to the activity of the devil, who comes to steal, kill, and destroy.[68] However, visions and dreams are the instruments of the fourth dimension. To Cho, believing the word of God to the point of imagining it to be true is key to healing. "If

---

[67] Cho, *Use Your Faith Energy*, 30.
[68] Park, "David Yonggi Cho and International Pentecostal/Charismatic Movements," 237.

the Christian takes the brush of faith and begins to paint on the canvas of his heart the pictures that God has revealed to him, those revelations become reality."[69] Oral Roberts did not emphasize the work of the mind. To him, what was important was seed faith, a point of contact, the Word of God, and faith.

c. The Power of Speech

Cho assigns great power to the spoken word of the believer. He is more in line with Kenneth Hagin's teaching on confessions, although he does not use that term as such. Although Roberts recommended believing, speaking, and acting to receive healing, he did not emphasize the teaching of Rhema, word of faith, or confessions as a major theme of his theology of healing.

d. Preventive Measures and Health Maintenance

Both Roberts and Cho have outlined spiritual disciplines to preserve divine healing. In terms of preventive measures, Roberts believed in the importance of physical exercise. In fact, aerobic exercise is required of all students at Oral Roberts University. But his theology of healing does not emphasize diet and exercise, as Cho's does. Cho writes considerably about preventive measures one can take to maintain health. These, as we have seen, include stress reduction, a healthy diet, and exercise.

A Difference in Articulation: Biblical versus Multidisciplinary Basis

Roberts was a highly intelligent, well-read man, but he developed his theology of healing in a traditional Pentecostal

---

[69] Cho, *The Fourth Dimension*, vol. 2, 52.

way. Even as he promoted whole-person medical practice, he was thoroughly biblical in his articulation of divine healing. Cho's theology was certainly biblical and revelational, but his articulation reflects several disciplines. He referred to science, psychology, and other fields of study. His theology of healing was more directly informed by other branches of learning. He talked about Albert Einstein's theory of relativity in his discussion of seed faith.[70] He referred to psychologists and neurosurgeons and philosophers in establishing his healing theology.[71] Roberts has had a tremendous influence on the fields of medicine and the healing arts. However, his theology is developed more directly from biblical history, themes, expositions, and revelations.

Oral Roberts and David Yonggi Cho were two great men whom God used to spread the message of the healing power of Jesus Christ across the world in the twentieth century. One was an American who was considered the foremost healing evangelist of the twentieth century. The other was an Asian who pastored the largest congregation in the world. Both experienced God's healing power personally during their youth. Both came from economically poor circumstances but caught a vision of the possibility of being blessed with salvation, health, and prosperity. Their theologies were truly Pentecostal/charismatic. Both men developed revolutionary concepts, such as seed faith, a point of contact, and the fourth dimension. Their healing ministries were motivated by their

---

[70] Cho, *The Fourth Dimension*, 3rd ed., 161.
[71] Cho, *The Fourth Dimension*, vol. 2, 89.

love for suffering humanity and their willingness to obey Jesus' command to preach, teach, and heal. Their lives and ministries have touched the body of Christ and the world. While there are differences in some of their theological constructs and emphases, both were practical theologians and practicing ministers with well-defined theologies of healing that could be characterized as biblical, Pentecostal, charismatic, and contextually appropriate.

Both Oral Roberts and Yonggi Cho have been criticized for some aspects of their teachings, but their major teachings on divine healing pass biblical scrutiny very well. As a person who was a part of Oral Roberts University for decades, I had abundant opportunities to observe Roberts's ministry closely. He was truly a healing evangelist who paid a high price for his stance on divine healing and had a very positive impact on healing ministry and medical practice globally. I also had the opportunity to meet Pastor Yonggi Cho personally and hear his perspective on pastoral and healing ministries. I have preached at Yoido church and at healing crusades held at Yoido's prayer mountain, which were sponsored by ORU DMin alumni in Korea. I had many helpful conversations with Mrs. Yonggi Cho, who holds a DMin degree from ORU, regarding her husband's healing ministry. I had candid and meaningful conversations about Cho's healing theology with several scholars, including the late Dr. Vinson Synan. I also interviewed several Yoido pastors, some of whom were ORU graduates, regarding the impact of Cho's healing ministry in Korea and beyond. I can testify that Cho's theology has had a lasting and positive impact on Korea and other nations.

I included the biographies and healing theologies of these globally well-known ministers with the hope that those readers who may have theological issues with their positions on blessing, seed faith, and so on would not summarily dismiss their valuable teachings on healing. Hopefully, readers will find the testimonies of these men as catalysts to develop their own theological positions that would embolden them to pray for healing for themselves and others.

CHAPTER 11

DOCTORS, HOSPITALS, AND THE HEALING LEGACY OF JESUS

Peter J. Floriani defines *hospital* as an "organized and complex system of highly trained professionals, having a wide variety of skills, all of which are aimed at identification and treatment and care of a suffering human being."[1] The root word for *hospital* relates to the concept of hospitality, and the word *clinic* is rooted in the Greek word *kline*, which means "bed," said Floriani.[2] We will briefly examine the history of this complex system called hospital to see the historic connection between modern hospitals and the compassion of Jesus.[3]

---

[1]   Peter J. Floriani, *An Introduction to the History of the Hospital* (n.p.: independently published, 2018), 11.

[2]   Floriani, 15.

[3]   This chapter contains information received from the lectures, class notes, and several conversations with the late Roger L. Youmans, MD, who was my co–teacher in a course called "Healing Team Concepts," which was required for fourth-year medical students at the former Oral Roberts University (ORU) School of Medicine. Written by Youmans and printed by the ORU Bookstore, *Healing Team Concepts Manual* was a course reader.

Ancient History

The documented history of humanity's work to heal the sick begins with the Code of Hammurabi, which was written around 1900 BC. This code recommended both religious and empiric treatments of patients and included clear ethical guidelines. Unethical physicians and those involved in malpractice were threatened with severe punishments. "A doctor's fee for curing a severe wound would be 10 silver shekels for a gentleman, five shekels for a freedman and two shekels for a slave. Penalties for malpractice followed the same scheme: a doctor who killed a rich patient would have his hands cut off, while only financial restitution was required if the victim was a slave."[4] Obviously, the fee for treating a patient was very high and beyond the reach of ordinary individuals, but it appears that various types of treatments were available then to the sick that could be considered specializations.

Historians say that Egyptian documents dating to 1700 BC describe certain surgical procedures in detail. Other documents, from 1600 BC, describe medications to be prescribed as well as religious incantations to be used.[5] The Egyptians treated the visible symptoms as well as dealt with the religious aspects of illness. Some treatments included drugs and sorcery.

According to *The Catholic Encyclopedia*, ancient hospitals appear to have existed in Ireland (the *Broin Bearg*, "House of Sorrow") in 300 BC and in India in 252 BC during King Ashoka's

---

[4] History.com editors, "Code of Hammurabi," *History*, November 9, 2009, https://www.history.com/topics/ancient-history/hammurabi.
[5] Youmans, *Healing Team Concepts Manual*, 27.

reign.[6] Similar institutions may have existed in Mexico. Based on available information, it is not possible to prove the existence of hospitals as we know them now in these ancient times, although the existence of efforts to alleviate suffering is abundantly clear. It is also clear that the medical work done in these places was connected to the religions of the respective regions.

It is believed that the earliest physicians were more like itinerant evangelists. They traveled with their instruments and pharmacies (herbs and pharmaceutical materials in bags) to the sick who could afford their services. The poor went to the temples for treatment.

Roger Youmans stated that there were distinctive practices of medical care in the world of the ancient Greeks. One form of treatment was requiring the patient to sleep in the temple, which involved taking drugs, bathing, and receiving massages. It was believed that while the patient slept, he could be visited by a god. This was called "incubation."[7] In a different model, drugs, physical therapy, rest, and religious expressions were used to bring about healing. Later, during the period 460–377 BC, Hippocrates of Cos (off the coast of modern Turkey) emerged as a healer. He is considered the father of modern medicine. Hippocrates relied on careful observation and reason instead of religious rituals. His writings and those of his followers (Aphoriums of Hippocrates, 150 BC) reflect issues of religious faith, but his medical work was based on observable data.

---

[6] Floriani, *An Introduction to the History of the Hospital*, 16.
[7] Floriani, 16.

The father of modern physicians believed that sickness was a natural process that was not related to religion, morality, or God's anger. Hippocrates focused on the patient's hygiene, nutrition, and exercise in relation to healing and well-being. He defined the physician as a practitioner of science, not a priest.[8] Diagnosis was based on observation, logic, and integrity. Hippocrates believed that the patient's atmosphere, not the treatment provided, played the most important role in his or her recovery. Even in the Greek world, only the rich could afford medical care.

Other noted centers of medical practice developed in Pergamum, Smyrna, Laodicea, and Ephesus, all parts of today's Turkey and very familiar to Bible readers. A well-known center of medicine in Alexandria, the ancient center of learning in Africa, produced the great Galen, who holds a celebrated place in the history of medicine.[9]

It is believed that among the ancient Romans, the head of the household treated sick family members with the help of slaves who had medicinal knowledge. The Romans provided societal support for healing, such as providing clean water made available through aqueducts and sewer systems to maintain environmental hygiene.[10] They employed individuals specially trained to treat the wounded in their armies. These individuals provided practical helps.[11] Similar facilities may have been

---

[8] Youmans, *Healing Team Concepts Manual*, 27.
[9] Floriani, *An Introduction to the History of the Hospital*, 18, referencing Thorndike, *History of Magic and Experimental Science*, 1:117–181.
[10] Youmans, *Healing Team Concepts Manual*, 28.
[11] Floriani, *An Introduction to the History of the Hospital*, 17, referencing "Medicine" 12–3, 25 in *The Oxford Classical Dictionary*, 550–51.

developed for the imperial officials and their families. There are remains of military hospitals in the Empire. The best ones were found in lower Germany (on the Rhine frontier) and Switzerland, where numerous medical instruments were found.[12]

Sadly, during all this history, the poor and the oppressed were almost always excluded or abandoned.[13] This situation changed only after the life, death, and resurrection of Jesus and the expansion of the Christian faith across the Roman Empire. One must not forget a physician by the Greek name Luke, who reported the healing work of Jesus in his first book and the continuing work of the apostle Paul in his second book, Acts of the Apostles. Paul called him "the beloved physician" (Col 4:14). Historian Gary B. Ferngren said that the medicine Luke practiced reflected the training and medical views he shared with his contemporaries in the Greco-Roman culture.[14] According to Floriani, Luke, along with well-known Syrian physicians and twin brothers/saints Cosmos and Damian, refused to accept payment for their services and were eventually martyred.

Hebrew and Greek Approaches

The Hebrews' approach to the sick and afflicted was fundamentally different from that of other nations and people. Their health and well-being revolved around their God and depended on their relationship with Him. Starting with the Passover, the Hebrews were instructed to depend on God and follow

---

[12] Floriani, 550–51.

[13] Youmans, *Healing Team Concepts Manual*, 29.

[14] Gary B. Ferngren, *Medicine and Health Care in Early Christianity* (Baltimore: Johns Hopkins University, 2009), 10.

His commandments to maintain their health and to receive healing when needed. They received this assurance at Marah: "If you diligently heed the voice of the LORD your God and do what is right in His sight, give ear to His commandments and keep all His statutes, I will put none of the diseases on you which I have brought on the Egyptians. For I am the Lord who heals you" (Exod 15:26).

The religious motivation behind the Jewish practice of medicine has been documented. According to H. Dubovsky, "Jewish interest in medicine has a religious motivation with the preservation of health and life as religious commandments in the Holy Scriptures. Despite a basic belief that God caused disease and effected cures with physicians as agents, Jews accepted the rational medicine of ancient Greece. They assisted in the spread of these teachings in the Roman and Arab empires but carried them to the rest of Europe in their migrations."[15]

Amazingly, modern science confirms the validity of the biblical admonitions. A healthy lifestyle does prevent diseases. Noticeably, the Hebrew priests were teachers of the health laws but not real practitioners of healing. The priests verified healing of the sick, but it appears that the prophets were the ones who were more involved with the healing work. The Hebrews had wound dressers, midwives, and physicians among them (Gen 35:17; 2 Chr 16:12). The Hebrew prophets taught that God was the center of their health and that a proper relationship with Him was the key to their well-being.

---

[15] H. Dubovsky, "The Jewish Contribution to Medicine, Part I. Biblical and Talmudic Times to the End of the 18th Century," *South African Medical Journal* 76, no. 1 (July 1, 1989): 26–8.

The Greek approach was more empirical and intellectual, seeing man as a two-part being with soul and body.[16] They saw the soul as good and the body as bad, all the while glorifying the body. The Hebrews, on the other hand, saw man as a unitary being, a living soul. Made from the dust of the earth, man was created in the image of God. A human being was neither a body with a spirit nor a spirit with a body, but a living soul with both body and spirit that could not be separated without making the person nonexistent. In the Hebrew understanding, human beings are whole persons with body, soul, and spirit. Jesus of Nazareth embodied this truth in His life and ministry, and Paul the apostle articulated it. Paul prayed for the Thessalonian believers, "Now may the God of peace Himself sanctify you completely; and may your whole spirit, soul, and body be preserved blameless at the coming of our Lord Jesus Christ" (1 Thess 5:23).

Jesus' Definition of Neighbor

Cultures and civilizations that existed before the establishment of the church did not value the lives of the sick. It was not uncommon to see chronically ill people abandoned by these societies. Although individuals who had families were cared for by their loved ones, those without relatives, and especially the poor, received practically no care at all. It is difficult for us to understand what a revolutionary Jesus was when it came to the acceptance and embracing of the sick and the afflicted in society.

---

[16] Youmans, *Healing Team Concepts Manual*, 30.

Ferngren reported, "Philanthropy among the Greeks did not take the form of private charity or of a personal concern for those in need, such as orphans, widows, or the sick. There was no religious or ethical impulse for almsgiving. . . . In contrast with the emphasis in Judaism on God as particularly concerned for the welfare of the poor, the Greek and Roman gods showed little pity on them; indeed, they showed greater regard for the powerful who could offer them sacrifices."[17] The Romans believed that human worth was something that had to be earned, but in Judaism and Christianity, human worth was intrinsic based on the fact that each individual is created in the image of God and therefore highly valuable.[18] This was the essence of Jesus' statement, "Assuredly, I say to you, inasmuch as you did it to one of the least of these My brethren, you did it to Me" (Matt 25:40).

The Gospels tell the story of Jesus as the healer and lover of those in the margins of society who taught to love not only God but also one's neighbor. His ideas were radical and shocking to His listeners. He challenged His followers to love their enemies and to do good to those who persecuted them. This was not a common teaching in those days, and it was not the ethics practiced by the leaders of religion or government at that time. Jesus got into trouble with the religious leaders of His day more often in relation to healing the sick or caring for the needy. He even broke the law regarding the Sabbath to do this.

---

[17] Ferngren, *Medicine and Health Care in Early Christianity*, 87.
[18] Ferngren, 95.

Jesus' definition of neighbor was truly radical. In Luke 10:29–37, the parable of the good Samaritan, He answered a lawyer's question about who his neighbor was. Here's a summary of that story: A man went on a journey. Thieves attacked him, robbed him, and fled. The wounded man was left helpless. A Jewish priest came by and saw the bleeding man, but he did not respond to his need. He showed no concern for this man as he continued his journey. Then along came a Levite, who also saw the man in need but walked on without intervening. The third person to come by was a Samaritan, one who did not represent the mainstream of society. He saw the wounded man and had compassion on him. He cared for the man, dressed his wounds, and carried him on his donkey to an inn where he could receive further care. The good Samaritan prepaid the innkeeper to take care of the wounded traveler and promised further payment for any additional expenses upon his return. The Samaritans were not a symbol of goodwill or dignity when Jesus shared this parable. His questioner had to admit that the Samaritan who showed mercy to the helpless man was the true "neighbor" to him.

Jesus' concept of neighbor was a radical and paradigm-shifting idea. Roger Youmans pointed out that the parable of the good Samaritan turned the question from "Who is my neighbor?" to "To whom am I a neighbor?"[19] Jesus changed the focus from the neighbor out there to the listener who is to be a neighbor. He taught that every person is a neighbor to any person in need. It is our responsibility to consider the

---

[19] Youmans, *Healing Team Concepts Manual*, 33.

person who may be wounded, sick, or in need and do what we can to help, even when the person in need is unfamiliar to us. Strangers and foreigners are our neighbors.

Imagine a society where the sick and the disabled were outcasts, expected to be out of sight and out of mind, where Jesus came with the teaching that the outcast is one's neighbor. Jesus was fulfilling His messianic anointing: "The Spirit of the LORD is upon Me," He said, "because He has anointed Me to preach the gospel to the poor; He has sent Me to heal the brokenhearted, to proclaim liberty to the captives and recovery of sight to the blind, to set at liberty those who are oppressed" (Luke 4:18). Jesus not only taught it in theory but practiced it and commanded His followers to go and do likewise. That command became a clarion call for the church through the centuries to care for the sick and afflicted and the needy.

It is this legacy of healing that the church inherited and continued to practice after the resurrection and the ascension of Jesus. His life and the example of the church influenced the surrounding cultures to consider taking care of the sick as a social and ethical responsibility. However, the dominant empires, civilizations, and cultures did not adapt this admonition easily or immediately. But thankfully, led by the church, changes did come. One can only imagine the plight of the sick had Jesus not come and the church not followed His teaching and example. This is why, even though there are medical practitioners who do not value the power of faith and prayer, one should not consider medical science and hospitals as enemies of divine healing. It was not medical science that first discredited the biblical teaching of healing. The church led the way in this plight.

The epistle of James commanded the elders of the church to pray for the sick and expect healing (5:14). The church has obeyed this command throughout its history, although at times the practice missed the hope and the promise of healing given in James's exhortation. We are called to minister healing to the sick and leave the timing of healing and whether it is naturally or supernaturally accomplished to God. Ours is to obey the command of the Lord Jesus Christ: heal the sick. In faith and obedience, the elders and believers must continue this practice of prayer that requires a willingness to let God be God.

Christians of the first three centuries were a persecuted group of Jesus-followers. They were known for their unique faith and practice. They drew the attention of their contemporaries through their willingness to believe in the resurrected Christ, their love for one another, and their compassion toward the sick and afflicted of society. This situation changed drastically in the fourth century, when Christianity became the official religion of the Roman Empire. The church enjoyed the newly received earthly acceptance and conformed in many ways to the values of the Roman culture and civilization. As the Roman royalty became Christians, the church's attention turned away from the things of God to the powers and accomplishments of this world. The church's view of healing changed significantly during this period, which began with the conversion of Emperor Constantine in the fourth century, but, as we have seen, the work of healing continued.

Hospitals: A Christian Legacy

Christianity promoted the care of the poor and sick and inspired the establishment of hospitals. Basil the Great, the Eastern father, founded most likely the first hospital for the poor in AD 372 near Caesarea.[20] This institution was part of a mega-charitable project involving care for lepers and other sick persons, with separate areas provided for the treatment of contagious and noncontagious patients. Both physicians and priests were involved in the care of the sick at Caesarea. This facility accepted physicians and medicines as God's servants for His healing work.

James J. Walsh in *The Catholic Church and Healing* quoted Gregory of Nazienzus regarding Basil's work: "It would be reckoned among the miracles of the world so numerous were the poor and sick that came hither and so admirable was the care and order with which they were served. . . . Before the gates of Caesarea called by Basil out of nothing rose a new city devoted to works of charity and to nursing the sick. Well built and furnished houses . . . contained the rooms for the sick and infirm of every variety who were entrusted to the care of doctors and nurses."[21]

Although Christianity promoted the care and healing of the sick, Christians held opposing views about medical care and hospitals throughout the ages. While Basil provided medical

---

[20] Floriani, *An Introduction to the History of the Hospital*, 21. See Morton Kelsey, *Healing and Christianity: A Classic Study* (New York: HarperCollins, 1976), 167.

[21] James J. Walsh, *The Catholic Church and Healing* (New York: MacMillan, 1928), 21. See also Floriani, *An Introduction to the History of the Hospital*, 21.

care along with spiritual care for the sick, Benedict of Nursia, the founder of the Benedictine Order who lived in the late fifth and early sixth centuries, on the other hand, forbade the study of medicine.[22] He believed that only prayer and divine intervention could heal diseases. Ministering to the sick was considered a major responsibility, but the monasteries offered the sick mostly prayers and supportive care. Later, when monks began to study medicine, that was prohibited by the church because medical practice brought them money on the side.[23]

While the official church and theologians differed in their views of healing, ordinary Christians were involved in the work of healing through medicine and prayer. Lady Fabiola, a wealthy Roman widow who inherited great wealth from her deceased second husband, as part of her penitential work, established a hospital at Porto (Ostia) on the mouth of the Tiber in Rome as early as AD 395.[24] She not only provided care for the sick in Rome but traveled widely to bring the sick and needy from distant places to the hospital. She also hired "traveling priests" who brought both Christian and non-Christian patients to the hospital. She brought in both free citizens and slaves.

Floriani mentioned two other early hospitals: one founded by Ephrem "the Deacon" in Edessa, now called Urfa, in Syria, and another founded around AD 400 by John Chrysostom in Constantinople, where he was bishop.[25] The monasteries continued this tradition of hospitality, taking care of the

---

[22] Youmans, *Healing Team Concepts Manual*, 50.
[23] Kelsey, *Healing and Christianity*, 210.
[24] Floriani, *An Introduction to the History of the Hospital*, 20.
[25] Floriani, 21.

travelers (stranger-guests, who in those days, did not have any comfortable means of transport, especially the poor) and the ill. Saint Benedict commanded the monks in his Rule to "relieve the lot of the poor" and "visit the sick." It is hard to determine the exact nature of the medical attention the monks provided, but according to Floriani, two historical facts are evident: (1) the monks took care of the poor and the travelers and did not turn away anyone due to cost, and (2) they maintained libraries, transcribing available books on medical knowledge and leaving a legacy for the advancing field of medicine.

Other religious orders took up similar work. The Hospitallers of Saint John of Jerusalem, also known as the Knights of Rhodes and the Knights of Malta, is one example. This order had three classes: the military brothers, the infirmarians, and the chaplains. They were not motivated by material rewards, as all of them took the monastic vows and the last group was made up of ordained priests. There was a corresponding order of women called the Order of Saint Mary Magdalene who provided care for the pilgrim women who came to Jerusalem. Another order was the Brothers of the Holy Ghost. A branch of this order, the Hospitallers of the Holy Ghost, was founded at Montpellier, France, in 1180. These religious orders were instrumental in the development of hospitals as we know them.[26]

Similar establishments were functioning outside the monasteries. The *xanodochiam* (a place-to-receive-strangers) called *Hotel-Dieu* (guesthouse of God) was one of them built in Lyons, France, by King Childebert. *The Catholic Encyclopedia* describes

---

[26] Floriani, 28.

the Hotel-Dieu at Paris (dating back to 660 AD) with these words: "Soldiers and citizens, religious and laymen, Jews and Mohammedans, repaired in case of need to the *Hotel-Dieu*, and all were admitted, for all bore the marks of poverty and wretchedness; there was no other requirement."[27]

One thing is sure. All these efforts were based on their understanding of the words of Jesus: "For I was hungry and you gave Me food; I was thirsty and you gave Me drink; I was a stranger and you took Me in. . . . Assuredly, I say to you, inasmuch as you did it to one of the least of these My brethren, you did it to Me" (Matt 25:35, 40). They were also motivated by the warning given to those who who disregard the rules of the kingdom of God: "But the sons of the kingdom will be cast out into outer darkness. There will be weeping and gnashing of teeth" (8:12).

The same motivation caused Saint Francis of Assisi (1181/82–1226) to embark on his mercy work by embracing a leper. Likewise, Saint Catherine of Siena (1347–1380) cared, with her own hands, for the lepers and those with terrible illnesses and horrible wounds whom others refused to touch. Floriani presented additional examples. The Sisters of Charity, founded by Saint Vincent de Paul (1581–1660) and Saint Louise de Marillac, combined religious life with care for the sick. Saint Vincent believed in prayer and medicine and founded several hospitals. Saint Peter Canisius (1521–1597) "relied most on prayer" but defended those who used the

---

[27] From "Hospitals" in *The Catholic Encyclopedia*, quoting Coyecque, *L'Hotel–Dieu de Paris au Paris au Moyen Age*, I, 63. See also Floriani, *An Introduction to the History of the Hospital*, 27.

weapons of science (medicine and hospitals). There is a story about Saint John of God (1495–1550), who built a hospital in Granada, where he saved several patients during a fire in the hospital by carrying them on his back, passing through the flames several times somehow unhurt.[28]

The legacy of Florence Nightingale (1820–1910) as the lady with the lamp sheds light on the contributions of nurses to the care and healing of the sick, motivated by their faith. The motivating power behind Nightingale, who professionalized nursing, and other pioneering nurses was Christian faith and Christ's call to compassion. Today that legacy continues all over the world, and it is not limited to Christian institutions.

It is evident that Christian medical care has impacted the world in profound ways. From David Livingstone to the most recent missionary physician, the world has been blessed with people who offer unselfish and compassionate medical care in the name of Jesus Christ. Their work should not be a hindrance to praying for the sick in the name of the One who is the author and finisher of their faith (Heb 12:2). The work of physicians, nurses, and hospitals bears witness to the truth that God is concerned about the sick and that He heals naturally and supernaturally. Unfortunately, most hospitals, including many Christian institutions, and a lot of Christians have forgotten this legacy.

Natural and the Supernatural

God is at work in the world, and He heals naturally and supernaturally. Sincere efforts to heal the sick using natural

---

[28] See Floriani, *An Introduction to the History of the Hospital*, 61–62.

means is not a hindrance to God's supernatural work of healing in and out of the hospital. I have seen healings attributable to the supernatural work of God during my chaplaincy work at the City of Faith Hospital in Tulsa, Oklahoma. I have seen what can only be described as miracles in the medical as well as specialized units of the hospital on several occasions during my seven years of ministry there. Two incidents stand out.

The first involved Lindsay Roberts, Oral Roberts's daughter-in-law. She was admitted to the City of Faith Hospital as a surgery patient. People of faith around the country prayed for her, and I visited her as a chaplain, as she was in my assigned area of responsibility. On the day of the surgery, her husband, Richard (before he was president of the university), was with her as I visited them. Before she was taken to the surgical suite, Richard and I joined in a prayer of faith for her.

I kept an eye open to see her returning after surgery but was surprised to see her come back just a short time after leaving the room. I was told that she did not need the surgery, as the doctors could not find the previously identified tumor that was supposed to be removed. I heard Lindsay's public testimony later, in which she stated that if that surgery had been done, she would not be the proud mother of three daughters today!

The second story involved a patient with a very large tumor on her neck. Dr. Gene Koelker was my colleague and the chaplain where this patient was. One day he called me and other chaplains to join him in his area to pray for a new patient. It was our protocol to call colleagues to join us for prayer when we faced particularly difficult situations, so it was not unusual to receive such a call. When a call like that came, all we knew was that the chaplain who had made the call had run into a difficult situation and needed personal and ministry support from colleagues. Some of us joined Dr. Koelker that day in the patient's room. I noticed that the female patient had a very large tumor on her neck. I had never seen a tumor that big. It was almost as large as her face, such that she could not look down! I was getting distracted by the size of the tumor and was moved by the helpless look on the patient's face. Dr. Koelker read a passage from the Bible and anointed the patient with oil and invited us to join him in prayer. (All chaplains at the City of Faith carried small vials of anointing oil to pray for the sick according to James 5:14.) We put all our trust in God and joined in a prayer for healing. Nothing looked different as the prayer ended, except that there was a ray of hope on the patient's face. We went back to our respective areas as Dr. Koelker continued his conversation with the patient.

The next morning we received another call from Chaplain Koelker, asking us to join him in the same patient's room. I was surprised to be called again to the same room but responded. I could not believe what I witnessed in the room. The large tumor was completely gone! Overnight, the tumor had fully disappeared. There was no evidence of it left behind except for some loose skin around the patient's neck. I do not know what type of medicine was given to her. Neither do I know if I witnessed a miracle of medicine, prayer, or both. All I knew was that I had never seen anything like that tumor disappear that fast. We joined Chaplain Koelker, the patient, and her nurse and thanked God in prayer. I remember the patient being full of joy. She was discharged a few days later.

True science should not be an enemy of God, for the ultimate purpose of science must be to discover the glory of God. Medical science should not be the enemy of faith in God and prayer. Although the prayer of faith can heal the sick without any medical intervention, prayer and medicine should not be against each other. They should complement each other. Unfortunately, modern medicine as the multibillion-dollar industrial complex involving the medical establishment, pharmaceutical giants, and insurance monopolies in many ways has left the sick and their concerns behind. Still, receiving medical care should not be a hindrance to praying for healing by faith.

Does God Want to Empty All Hospital Beds?

Some who believe in divine healing argue that God will always heal everyone, and they present many biblical texts to support this claim. This group includes many who believe that people of faith should not trust physicians or seek medical care, as these are indications of a lack of faith in God. Some have tried to or, in few cases, claimed that they emptied hospital wards through prayer alone. It is important to assess this matter from a biblical perspective.

Matthew told us that Jesus healed every disease: "And Jesus went about all Galilee, teaching in their synagogues, preaching the gospel of the kingdom, and healing all kinds of sickness and all kinds of disease among the people. Then His fame went throughout all Syria; and they brought to Him all sick people who were afflicted with various diseases and torments, and those who were demon-possessed, epileptics, and paralytics; and He healed them. . . . Then Jesus went about all the cities and villages, teaching in their synagogues, preaching the gospel of the kingdom, and healing every sickness and every disease among the people" (4:23–24; 9:35). Matthew also reported that *all* who touched Jesus were healed (14:34–36). Scholars discuss the translation issues related to "every kind" and "every" in Matthew. Many conclude that the emphasis is on the variety of illnesses rather than on the number of ill people.

Mark appears to have been more cautious in his descriptions, saying that Jesus healed *many*, implying *not all:* "At evening, when the sun had set, they brought to Him all who were sick and those who were demon-possessed. And the whole city was gathered together at the door. Then He healed many who were sick with various diseases" (1:32–34). Mark 3:10 tells us again that Jesus "healed many, so that as many as had afflictions pressed about Him to touch Him." He used similar language in the sixth chapter also: "Wherever He entered, into villages, cities, or the country, they laid the sick in the marketplaces, and begged Him that they might just touch the hem of His garment. And as many as touched Him were made well" (v. 56). This again implied that many were healed but not necessarily all who were brought to Him.

The level of faith in the patients or in those who brought them to Jesus were factors in the reported cases of healing in all the Gospels. Luke follows Matthew's pattern of presenting Jesus as healing all as well as healing many (not all):

A great multitude of people from all Judea and Jerusalem, and from the seacoast of Tyre and Sidon . . . came to hear Him and be healed of their diseases, as well as those who were tormented with unclean spirits. And they were healed. And the whole multitude sought to touch Him, for power went out from Him and healed them all. . . . And that very hour He cured many of infirmities, afflictions, and evil spirits; and to many blind He gave sight. (Luke 6:17–19; 7:21)

In chapters 9 and 10, Luke stated or implied that all needing healing or all in a particular town were healed. "[Jesus] went aside privately into a deserted place belonging to the city called Bethsaida. But when the multitudes knew it, they followed Him; and He received them and spoke to them about the kingdom of God, and healed those who had need of healing. . . . Then He said to them, . . . 'Whatever city you enter . . . heal the sick there, and say to them, "The kingdom of God has come near to you"'" (9:10–11; 10:2, 8–9). The story of the ten lepers in Luke 17:12–19 is another occasion of a whole group being healed.

According to John's Gospel, although there were many disabled people by the pool of Bethesda, Jesus healed only one (5:2–9). The book of Acts follows the pattern of Luke's Gospel. While all were healed in Acts 5:16, many were healed in Acts 8:6–8. Later, in Paul's writings, both the account of Trophimus being left behind in Miletus sick (2 Tim 4:20) and Epaphroditus becoming sick almost unto death (see Phil 2:25–27) indicated that God's servants in good relationship with Him also can suffer from illness. We do not know the final outcome of Trophimus's illness, but we do know that God had mercy on Epaphroditus and he was restored.

We can conclude that God is a healer. He heals, but He does not heal everyone in all situations and at all times by our calendar. God is sovereign, and His healing work must be seen in light of His plans and purposes. The cases in which the prayer for healing did not or does not produce the expected results in terms of outcome or timing should not prevent us from praying for healing. They should only encourage us to pray for the sick by faith in the name of Jesus and expect healing with the understanding that all of life is under the sovereignty of a loving God. This approach may not empty all hospital beds but will result in many experiencing God's gift of healing, some instantly, some gradually, some naturally, some supernaturally, and all ultimately at the resurrection.

Holistic Medicine versus Whole-Person Medicine

It is easy to confuse the concepts of holistic medicine and whole-person medicine. Strictly speaking, whole-person healing is a biblical and Christian concept whereas, although some Christian practitioners still use the term *holistic*, this concept is more secular and spiritually syncretic. While whole-person healing is related to the biblical concept of wholeness, holistic healing as normally understood and practiced does not scrutinize its methods from a Christian theological perspective. Whole-person healing considers the sick person's body, mind, and spirit from a Judeo-Christian perspective. Other dimensions of a person's life, such as relationships and finances, may also be considered. The biblical idea of wholeness is related to the theological idea of sanctification or holiness. A statement

I heard from Oral Roberts expresses this connection: "Wholeness is holiness and holiness is wholeness." Wholeness from a biblical perspective is not perfection. It is a dynamic way of being well even when everything is not perfect in one's life, based on faith in the promises of God in Jesus Christ.

Holistic healing, on the other hand, is not necessarily based on a Christian worldview or a Christian understanding of person and personal wholeness. For instance, there are holistic healers who believe in healing through auras, crystals, spells, and charms. Globally speaking, some healing practitioners treat their patients with magic and witchcraft and call it holistic healing work. Yoga practices accompanied by non-Christian religious exercises and mind-emptying meditation (as opposed to Christian meditation) are used by some holistic practitioners. Hypnosis is practiced as a holistic healing method. Touch therapy with no direct link to the biblical instruction regarding laying of hands on the sick also is a part of mainstream holistic healing work today. There are also those among holistic healers who administer exorcisms from a non-Christian religious understanding.

Extra-natural healing can take place outside Christian faith and ministry. There is biblical precedent for this phenomenon. Signs, wonders, and miracles were performed by those outside the Hebrew and Christian traditions in biblical times. Moses and Aaron performed miracles to demonstrate Yahweh's authority to demand the release of the Hebrew slaves in Egypt. The Egyptian magicians were able to match their work initially. Aaron's staff became a serpent when he dropped it, but so did the Egyptians' rods. Although Moses and Aaron were able to outperform the opposing magicians, as Aaron's rod swallowed up all the other rods dropped by the Egyptian magicians and sorcerers, the fact remains that miracles took place outside the power of the God of Abraham, Isaac, and Jacob.

Likewise, in the New Testament, Simon the magician was a man with a tremendous ability to perform miracles: "But there was a certain man called Simon, who previously practiced sorcery in the city and astonished the people of Samaria, claiming that he was someone great, to whom they all gave heed, from the least to the greatest, saying, 'This man is the great power of God.' And they heeded him because he had astonished them with his sorceries for a long time" (Acts 8:9–11). Paul told the Corinthian believers that Satan himself masquerades as an angel of light (2 Cor 11:14 NIV). And the words of Jesus in Matthew 7:22–23 should be of great concern even to Christian healing ministers who consider themselves sound in doctrines and authorized by God to minister healing. He said, "Many will say to Me in that day, 'Lord, Lord, have we not prophesied in Your name, cast out demons in Your name, and done many wonders in Your name?' And then I will declare to them, 'I never knew you; depart from Me, you who practice lawlessness!'" Practitioners of Christian healing ministry must always be engaged in self-examination to make sure they are in right relationship with the Lord Jesus Christ and that they are following the promptings of His Spirit in responding to people's needs.

Some Conclusions

Hospitals are a testimony to the healing legacy of Jesus and His church. Doctors and nurses are not agents of the devil.

Hospitals are not a hindrance to divine healing. Despite all the problems plaguing the medical industrial complex, one must admit that hospitals exist to help the sick and to promote healing.

Doctors cannot heal. They can only offer their knowledge and skills to help the sick and promote healing. In this sense, they are ministers of healing who use natural means developed by the scientific method. People who pray for the sick are ministers of healing who use spiritual means of faith and prayer drawn from the deep wells of Christian spirituality. Healing can happen naturally and supernaturally. God can use both natural and supernatural means of healing. One approach can enhance the other, especially when there is a desire for whole-person health.

All doctors depend on the healing capacity built into the human being by God. God is not limited by natural laws, and He does not need natural means to bring about healing and wholeness, but God usually employs natural means and works within the laws of nature. The prayer of faith is efficacious at the church and at the hospital. Prayer in the name of Jesus Christ offered by faith is a powerful and potent instrument of healing.

CHAPTER 12

CESSATIONISM, PROSPERITY GOSPEL, AND PENTECOSTAL OVERREACTION

As we have seen in the previous historical sections, there have always been individuals and communities that have struggled with the idea of divine healing. There have been more such strugglers in the Western church. Unable to endorse the record of the Scripture or believe the claims of Christ at face value due to their philosophical orientation and the resulting worldview, many have tried to deal with the incidents of healings and miracles in the Bible simply as metaphoric, not relevant to modern believers in any real sense. Others tried to confine the biblical incidents to a dispensational period at the beginning of the Christian faith.

There have been different ways and means to discount whatever the enlightened skeptics considered nonessential to the Christian faith, even though this is not an easy thing to do, especially because, at the end of the day, one must deal with an event called the resurrection that took place at a real place in real time and is quintessential to Christian faith of any kind. Nevertheless, the skeptics' voices dominated mainstream Christianity for a very long time. Meanwhile, believers in divine healing throughout history have been variously admired, abused, excommunicated, marginalized, and ignored, but the practice of divine healing never went away from the church, although at times the carriers of the message of healing have been considered unorthodox in some ways.

Cessationists

Many scholars have tried to cope with the challenges against their Christian faith raised by certain scientists, philosophers, and university systems through various forms of higher criticism. Some have even turned the resurrection of Jesus into a simple metaphor for renewed life in the world. Brilliant theological minds from the days of early Western church fathers have struggled to cope with the certainty of the promises of God within His divine sovereignty, looking for airtight doctrines of healing that conform strictly to all the natural laws and, at the same time, guarantee predictable positive outcomes to all who seek healing. Generally called *cessationists*, these strugglers have put forth many reasons why the sick should not believe in divine healing in this age of science, technology, and advanced civilization. Following are some of these reasons:

1. Healing and miracles took place in the first and second centuries as the church was being established and Scripture was being written and codified. By the mid-second

century, the Scriptures had been completed, and there was no need anymore for supernatural occurrences to establish or guide the church. We should now be guided by the Scripture. As that which is full (Scripture) has come, we no longer need the partial (healing). We now have full knowledge through the Word of God, and the partial has passed away.

2. Sin is the cause of illness, and God uses illness to chastise His beloved children. Therefore, there is no need to pray for or expect healing. Instead, the sick should endure God's chastisement patiently.

3. Sickness and suffering can sanctify the Christian. Perseverance in sickness is the way to holiness.

4. Every believer has been assigned a cross to bear in this life. Sickness is a cross to bear.

5. Signs and wonders were essential to the preaching of the kingdom of God in the first century. They confirmed the truthfulness and authenticity of the gospel during the time of Jesus and His disciples. The message of the kingdom of God has been preached and established. There remains no need to pray for or expect any signs, wonders, healings, or miracles.

6. Primitive people believed in miracles and needed them for validation of truth. The modern/postmodern world and its inhabitants do not have a need for miracles. Belief in the existence of the supernatural itself reflects a primitive mindset.

7. Belief in the existence of demons is another remnant of primitive thinking and worldview. Evil does exist in

the world, but there is no personified evil, like Satan or the devil.

8. No ordinary person can minister healing. Only saints can pray for healing. Ordinary Christians should not expect answers to their prayers for healing.

9. Ordinary Christians do not have the amount of faith required to receive healing through prayer.

10. Some unusual individuals may have a special gift of healing, but ordinary believers need not pray for the sick or expect healing.

11. All healing ministers are crooks. Their prayers are only manipulations to collect money from their sick victims.

12. Modern medicine has given us many miracle drugs and treatment procedures. There is no need to believe in divine healing or pray for the sick today.

At the root of all these reasons is modern/postmodern Christians' struggle to believe the authentic record of the supernatural in the biblical narrative and to see its relevance to the life of the current church. They do not want to address the mega question this raises: What is Christianity devoid of the supernatural? After the virgin birth, the life and ministry of Jesus, and ultimately the resurrection of Jesus, did the Almighty put Himself in a time capsule? This is really a tough place to be, but that is the very place where many Christians are today.

Some cessationists discount all modern healing ministries, claiming they come not from the Holy Spirit, but from a strange fire. John MacArthur, for example, has written many books reflecting this philosophy. His *Strange Fire* was a strong attack, but it contained pretty much the same reasons I already mentioned. R. T. Kendall's response to MacArthur came as a book titled *Holy Fire*. He addressed every argument MacArthur made. I highly recommend Kendall's book to all believers and skeptics.

Ultimately one must believe the Bible as the Word of God and interpret it with reverence. One must accept that Christianity truly is a faith that deals with the natural and the supernatural. Our limited understanding of God's creation through modern science should not be the final redactor of the things of God. Even after all the arguments and theological gymnastics, there is no way for a person to become a Christian without taking a leap of faith. A Christian faith that has no room for the supernatural in this life is a disabled faith. If God is at work in the world today, He should not be limited to our preconceived notions and dimensions.

A gospel that offers hope only in the world to come and not in this world is not the Christianity of the Bible. The good news that Jesus preached dealt with both this world and the world to come and the natural and the supernatural. The faith Timothy was instructed to preach and Peter advised his readers to follow offered hope for both this life and the life to come. Paul told Timothy, "For bodily exercise profits a little, but godliness is profitable for all things, having promise of the life that now is and of that which is to come" (1 Tim 4:8). Peter said, "Grace and peace be multiplied to you in the knowledge of God and of Jesus our Lord, as His divine power has given to us all things that pertain to life and godliness, through the knowledge of Him who called us by glory and virtue" (2 Pet 1:2–3). Divine healing through natural and supernatural means is, and must be, a part of the good news of Jesus Christ and therefore a practice of the followers of Jesus.

Fake Healers and Extreme-Prosperity Preachers

Some practitioners of divine healing have given abundant reasons for general skeptics and cessationists to affirm their anti-healing and anti-signs-and-wonders claims. Chief among them are some who have branded themselves as healing evangelists, initially in the United States and now globally, who have conducted themselves in scandalous ways. Disgraceful practices exposed have included fake healing reports, unethical handling of sick persons seeking help, claims of supernatural spiritual powers using hidden technologies, corrupt fundraising practices, and a lack of self-control with regard to their sexual behavior and/or handling of money. While there is a host of genuine servants of God who faithfully, sacrificially, and with compassion minister to the sick, the high-profile cases of a few exposed by secular media and other critics and spiritual vigilantes have created a lingering cloud of suspicion and mistrust that threatens to discredit the vital ministry of prayer and faith.

Oral Roberts documented numerous cases of healing that took place in his tent crusades long before he opened the City of Faith Hospital. He brought many of those healings, especially some of the spontaneous healings, to American living rooms through his TV programs. It is not well known that he instructed the people for whom he prayed to continue to follow their doctors' advice until they were healed and to seek confirmation of healing by their respective doctors. He was a very public figure who had the number one syndicated religious TV program in America for many years and, as noted in chapter 8, was considered one of the twentieth century's top two religious figures. Roberts was happily married for more than six decades and was never involved in any moral failures or scandals. (After raising hundreds of millions of dollars to build and operate a university and a two-million-square-foot medical complex, Roberts walked away from the ORU campus, taking nothing and making no financial claims, trusting God for his future, and placing the university in the hands of its legally rightful governing bodies. I was there, in the Holy Spirit Room, on that day and bore witness to his final statement to the faculty and administrators.) However, some have stretched his teachings on healing and giving and joined the disreputable group I just mentioned. This is especially true of those who are referred to as *extreme-prosperity preachers*.

There is a group of charismatic preachers who promote what is called *extreme-prosperity gospel*. This theology teaches that God wants His children to take charge of this world now and that He wants to bless them—primarily materially—above all others in the world. Some of them teach that the kingdom of God has fully come already and that we can live in that fullness now. They focus their teachings exclusively on physical health, material wealth, and other this-worldly blessings as the main benefits of faith in Christ. Some among them teach or strongly imply that if people will only have enough faith and follow certain steps, they can avoid all sufferings in this world and become as rich as they wish. They provide what can be seen as guaranteed biblical formulas or keys to gain health, wealth, and success without any serious mention of salvation, sanctification, discipleship, and spiritual growth.

This made-in-America doctrine has invaded the world. Many pastors I have met outside the United States testify that it causes much chaos in their poorer nations. Some who have embraced this theology in the majority world suffer from disillusionment and self-blame for not "having enough faith," according to these pastors and others. This is especially grievous in cases where the extreme-prosperity preachers, who dwell in the lap of luxury, require sacrificial donations from the poorest of the poor in the world. In effect, these preachers have made Oral Roberts's teaching on giving a fundraising tactic, dealing only with money (not time, talent, etc.) and the preacher's budget (not any other ministry or need).

God is indeed a good God. He wants to bless His people in all areas of their lives. However, the benefits of the gospel cannot be reduced to a list of earthly advantages and material possessions. The kingdom of God cannot be equated to some earthly nation and its political power. The Bible is clear: "My kingdom is not of this world" (John 18:36). "Our citizenship is in heaven" (Phil 3:20). "Seek ye first the kingdom of God, and his righteousness" (Matt 6:33 KJV). Suffering and death are part of the fallen world in which we live now. The afflictions of the righteous are many in this world, but the Lord will deliver His children from all of them (Ps 34:19). Christians have been redeemed from sin and death by Jesus' death on the cross of Calvary. God has given us forgiveness of sin and life everlasting, but Jesus did not come just to give us salvation for our souls. He said, "I have come that [you] may have life, and that [you] may have it more abundantly" (John 10:10). How can we limit abundant life to the condition of one's spirit alone? Jesus came with good news to the poor and the afflicted. How can we ignore His promise to bind up the brokenhearted (see Isa 61:1; Luke 4:18)? How can we ignore Peter's affirmation that by Christ's stripes "you were healed" (1 Pet 2:24)? God does heal the sick.

Likewise, good news to the poor cannot be that they will be poor forever (see again Luke 4:18). According to Paul, God will supply all our needs (Phil 4:19). This means that God answers prayers regarding needs other than salvation. There is such a thing called the "gospel lift," which shows that societies experience improvement when the gospel is preached. (Compare the status of education and women's health in areas with Christian influence against non-Christian areas in developing nations.) Unfortunately, many prosperity preachers are stretching the good news of Jesus—of salvation and provision—to the extreme until it becomes a lie and, unlike Oral Roberts, disregard God's sovereignty.

Some folks blame Oral Roberts for the spread of the extreme-prosperity gospel because of the aforementioned teaching he developed and popularized called "seed faith," which teaches (based on Philippians 4:14–19) that giving is the way to receiving and that one can develop a lifestyle of giving and receiving. As we have seen elsewhere, he had also developed a concept called the "point of contact," which he taught could release a person's faith to receive from God. He included seed faith as only one of several points of contact, such as time, talent, and so on, that a person could use. It appears that some of Roberts's imitators around the world have really stretched his teaching to a radical level.

I pointed this out to illustrate how this unbalanced teaching plays into the hands of those who do not believe in the current work of the Holy Spirit and are opposed to the ministry of healing. These ministers and their practices should not discredit the sound biblical practice of praying for the sick by faith. God heals and expects His church to practice the ministry of healing faithfully and with faith.

Lack of a Theology of Suffering

Another defense raised by cessationists is the argument that divine healing presupposes a Christian life free of suffering. They often point out that those who practice divine healing do not have an adequate theology of suffering. This is not necessarily true. While there are some who may practice healing ministry without sufficient theological reflection, this is not true of all believers and practitioners of divine healing. A balanced theology of suffering is not a hindrance to healing ministry. Many pastors and preachers outside the mainline churches are not formally educated in theology at higher levels. This may render them unable to articulate their theology clearly, but a biblically sound theology of suffering does not require higher learning or articulation if such a theology informs their practice. I recall Oral Roberts, a healing evangelist who was attacked by even some of his followers for opening a hospital, defending the opening of the City of Faith Hospital with these words: "It is appointed for man once to die. I am not trying to remove death from the world. I don't want anyone to die before their appointed time." Praying for healing is not the denial of the existence of real suffering in the world. It is an acknowledgment of the existence of suffering and a biblical effort to alleviate it.

I have attempted to articulate a theology of suffering that supports prayer of faith for healing. I will summarize the highlights of what I consider a Pentecostal/charismatic theology of suffering, articulated in my book *Ministry Between Miracles*,[1] to demonstrate that having a sound theology of suffering is not antithetical to believing in divine healing.

John Steely presented a biblical view in his translation of the book *Leiden* by E. S. Gerstenberger and W. Schrage.[2] The Old Testament does not give a uniform interpretation of suffering because suffering appears in many different forms and poses riddles that are too difficult.[3] Man has a tremendous need to fit suffering into his understanding of the structure of the world in some meaningful way, but suffering remains ambiguous.[4] In Old Testament thinking, Israel's one God is ultimately responsible for all the good and the bad in the universe; the presupposition is that, in some way, the sufferer himself gives impetus to his suffering. The Old Testament writers did not systematize the multiplicity of experiences, causes, and interpretations of suffering. They seemed to take

---

[1] See Mathew, *Ministry Between Miracles*, 113–35 (see chap. 9, n. 4).
[2] E. S. Gerstenberger and W. Schrage, *Suffering*, trans. John E. Steely (Nashville: Abingdon, 1980).
[3] Gerstenberger and Schrage, 103.
[4] Gerstenberger and Schrage, 103.

each calamity individually and attempted to deal with each pragmatically.

The Old Testament offers some comfort to the sufferer, in that the God of Israel suffered with His people. However, compared to the New Testament, it does not offer as a counterbalance to suffering a strong hope in the hereafter. This hope is offered when the New Testament completes the Old Testament. While the suffering of Jesus is central to the New Testament, the hope of resurrection, of life after death, provides a way to ultimately overcome suffering. Jesus did not engage in interpreting suffering but demonstrated that suffering could be borne and transcended—in fact, overcome. The vision of the suffering Christ viewed in the light of the resurrection yields the real meaning and the real comfort the sufferer needs.

The New Testament offers more than a message of ultimate healing and comfort—it also challenges the reader to engage in battling suffering in this earthly life. Therefore, the New Testament discusses suffering in the context of its mastery and conquest. The good news is that no suffering can separate us from the love of God in Jesus Christ.

E. Stanley Jones, the great missionary to India, dealt with this issue in his *Christ and Human Suffering*.[5] Jones saw suffering as a result of evil and said that there are two kinds of evil. The first evil is sin, which arises from within, from the choices of our will. The second evil comes from without, from our environment of society and the natural universe.

---

[5] E. Stanley Jones, *Christ and Human Suffering* (New York: Abingdon, 1933).

Jones lists nine avenues of suffering based on Luke 21:8–19:

1. sufferings from confused counsels in religion;
2. suffering from ways and conflicts in human society;
3. suffering from physical calamities in nature;
4. suffering from physical sickness and infirmities;
5. suffering from economic distress;
6. suffering from acts of one's own fellow men;
7. suffering from religious and secular authorities;
8. suffering through the home life; and
9. suffering from being associated with Christ.

Jones believed that only a solid Christian theology of the cross could adequately deal with the problem of suffering. God, in Jesus, suffered on the cross; God participated in human suffering at the cross, making the darkest hour of history the brightest. The end became the beginning—the cross became the throne! Jones proclaimed, "The Stoic bears, the Epicurean seeks to enjoy, the Buddhist and the Hindu stand apart, disillusioned, the Moslem submits, but only the Christian exults!"[6]

C. S. Lewis, in *The Problem of Pain*, suggested another aspect of pain in his idea that God uses pain as an instrument to call man to submit his will to Him. Lewis claimed a connection between the function of pain and God's purposes for man:[7] God whispers to us in our pleasures, speaks in our conscience, but shouts in our pains: it is His megaphone to

---

[6] Jones, 231.
[7] C. S. Lewis, *The Problem of Pain* (New York: Macmillan, 1962), 92–95.

rouse a deaf world, he said.[8] For Lewis, the real problem was "not why some humble, pious, believing people suffer, but why some do not."[9] Realizing the controversy of his position, he added, "I am not arguing that pain is not painful. Pain hurts. That is what the word means. I am only trying to show that the old Christian doctrine of being made 'perfect through suffering'" (Heb. 2:10) is not incredible."[10]

To Dietrich Bonhoeffer, the Christian theologian who was imprisoned and executed by the Nazis, "the useful theological question, then, does not arise about the origin of evil, but about the real overcoming of evil on the cross."[11] He continued, "The fact is that we live between the curse and the promise."[12] Both the pleasureful and the painful are a part of human life.

George Buttrick said, "We have to say that God *allows* pain from natural evil. We cannot say that he inflicts it."[13] God often enters our lives during times of natural calamity. "Pain turns our eyes from time to the mystery beyond time. So what we need is not an explanation, but a salvation."[14] Suffering is never objective, said Buttrick. An academic answer to suffering is sure to fail. The problem of suffering finds its answer as God enters our suffering. His entrance becomes our door of deliverance. God's suffering is a paradox, said

---

[8] Lewis, 93.
[9] Lewis, 104.
[10] Lewis, 104.
[11] Dietrich Bonhoeffer, *Creation and Fall* (1959; reprint ed., New York: Macmillan, n. d.), 76.
[12] Bonhoeffer, 83.
[13] George A. Buttrick, *God, Pain, and Evil* (Nashville: Abingdon, 1966), 45.
[14] Buttrick, 55.

Buttrick, one that can only be understood *in Jesus Christ*. Jesus His Son is the "breakthrough"—God's invasion of our history. Suffering begins to make sense in the light of the breakthrough event—the life, death, and resurrection of Jesus. Only those who believe and respond in faith can attain this understanding as they come to realize that natural evil, historical evil, and personal evil were conquered in this event: "The event of Christ has changed the bitter waters into a pool of healing."[15]

The alternatives to this perspective, such as stoicism and rebellion, sidestep the issue. The breakthrough in Christ, however, does not dispel the mystery of pain, since we do not know all about the snake in the original garden. Buttrick believed that pain can cause a cleansing from sin and the desire to sin. Pain cleanses from a false worldliness, lovelessness, self-centeredness, and even from the longing for a lost innocence and from subjugation to the dominion of time. Pain can give insights into the meaning of life, a new understanding of the natural world and human nature, and even a road toward understanding the nature of God.

We will never know just why this earth is destined to experience pain or why God should employ so strange a servant as the devil, but that ignorance is itself insight: "God's thoughts are not our thoughts, and his ways are not our ways."[16]

The event of the resurrection of Jesus Christ shows that suffering is transitory, parasitic, and temporary. Buttrick suggested that since pain and death are events, they cannot

---

[15] Buttrick, 125.
[16] Buttrick, 87.

be answered either by a formula in science or a theory in philosophy, but only understood in light of the life, death, and resurrection of Jesus!

It is clear that the Bible does not offer all the details about the origin of evil. This remains a mystery beyond human comprehension. We cannot fully understand this mystery because we are fallen people, sinners who have fallen and are falling. The fact is that evil exists alongside good in this world.

Mortal life must be viewed in the context of eternal life. Only the cross and the resurrection give true meaning to human suffering. Someday there will no longer be any suffering; only then will we understand fully the mystery of evil and suffering. By then, we will be fully redeemed, and the groaning of the whole creation will have ceased (see Rom 8:22). Meanwhile, we will live with the assurance that the "sufferings of this present time are not worthy to be compared with the glory which shall be revealed in us" (Rom 8:18).

I consider what I just highlighted as a good enough biblical perspective on suffering. I do not believe that having a sound theology of suffering somehow preempts praying for the sick in the name of Jesus. Jesus did not explain evil; He acknowledged its presence, confronted it with authority in His ministry, and triumphantly overcame it on the cross. Evil has been defeated, and Christ is alive to sustain that victory in our present time. It remains that we Christians are not exempt from all the laws of nature or the forces of evil during our lifetimes in this present world, but we have the privilege of praying by faith for deliverance from evil and suffering, including illness, even though the kingdom of God has not come fully yet.

Pentecostal Overreaction to the Extreme-Prosperity Gospel

I will conclude this section by mentioning a phenomenon I have observed within Pentecostalism in recent years, especially outside the United States, where the extreme-prosperity gospel has caused much havoc. I noticed a significant increase in this during the COVID-19 pandemic. Some online sermons preached in Pentecostal churches in India were eye-opening. It appears that pastors who lost members to the so-called new generation churches that teach extreme-prosperity gospel have decided to attack their competition by preaching that the only benefit one can expect from God in this age is salvation of the soul. Some of them preach that Christians should not expect healing or any other earthly help from God. There are preachers who hold this position as a badge of honor. I have heard sermons emphasizing that Timothy had stomach trouble, Trophimus was left sick in Miletus, Epaphroditus almost died from illness, and Paul's thorn in the flesh never left. These details are all true, but hearing Pentecostal preachers weighing them above all the signs, wonders, healings, miracles, and other ordinary provisions from God that are documented in the Gospels, Acts, and the Epistles and in the history of the modern Pentecostal/charismatic movement was a surprise to me.

I received a doctor of ministry research project proposal from a student in Asia who had lost many members of his church to extreme-prosperity teachers. Many of his remaining members were puzzled and disillusioned, and he had to help them through this time. His research proposal described the damage the extreme-prosperity gospel had done to the poor members of his church. Many are confused, condemning themselves for their lack of faith. Families are divided on the topic, some losing their faith in God completely. Unfortunately, his research plan was to present a gospel to them that offers only salvation for the soul, with no promise of any earthly help or healing in this life. He stated that the only healing one can expect is after death, at the resurrection. He quoted 2 Corinthians 1:20 in his paper this way: "All the spiritual promises of God in Him are Yes, and in Him Amen." The passage actually says, "For all the promises of God in Him are Yes, and in Him Amen, to the glory of God through us."

It appears that on the one hand, the evil one has used unethical healing ministers and preachers of extreme prosperity to discredit healing ministry through their excesses. On the other hand, he has driven Pentecostal preachers who wish to dissociate themselves from these unprincipled and misguided preachers, and who are overreacting to their excesses, to refuse to preach a gospel of salvation and healing that is relevant to the poor, sick, and marginalized. By making pastors ashamed enough to avoid preaching any message of God's provision for life and godliness, for this life and the life to come, the enemy has done significant damage. This is truly unfortunate. Jesus sent out His disciples to preach, teach, and heal: "Heal the sick, cleanse the lepers, raise the dead, cast out demons. Freely you have received, freely give" (Matt 10:8). The Pentecostal pioneers called it the "full gospel" and summarized it this way: Jesus saves. Jesus heals. Jesus baptizes in the Holy Spirit. And Jesus is coming soon. I hope the excesses of some ministers will not cause others to throw the whole truth about divine healing out. The antidote to wrong practice is not abandoning good practice; it is right practice. I hope there will always be Christians who acknowledge the existence of suffering even in the lives of the most faithful followers of Jesus but, at the same time, will not be ashamed or afraid to preach the whole counsel of God and pray for the sick by faith in the name of Jesus Christ.

CHAPTER 13

WHY I BELIEVE IN
MEDICINE AND PRAYER

I would like to conclude this book by summarizing our discoveries in the preceding chapters. I hope such a summary will concisely present my personal reasons for believing not only in natural healing, but also in divine healing. I hope my Christian readers—ministers, medical professionals, and all followers of Jesus—will see in these final pages their responsibility to pray for the sick by faith. And if *you* are in need of healing, I hope your faith in God will increase as a result of reading these pages.

The Bible

The key to health in the Hebrew Bible is a right relationship with God. The Old Testament promises healing to those who obey God. Sin is the root of sickness, but those who seek God can experience forgiveness and healing. The God of the Old Testament is a healer. He is a prayer-answering God. The

Old Testament provides laws and regulations to maintain health and to receive healing. The US Centers for Disease Control and Prevention (CDC) did not invent cleansing and quarantine to control the spread of diseases. The God of the Hebrews did.

The New Testament makes healing of the sick a matter of priority. The New Testament tells us that sin and sickness are connected but not every sickness is the result of the sick person's personal sin. The good news of Jesus Christ provides everlasting life, but it also offers help and hope for life in this world. The gospel promises both infinite hope and finite hope, hope in the life to come and hope for life in this world. As His Father was, Jesus was. He is the same yesterday, today, and forever (Heb 13:8).

Jesus was the divine healer. He healed the sick and asked His disciples to continue the ministry of healing. They were called to preach, teach, and heal. Healing is a sign of God's kingdom and a gift of the Holy Spirit. The gospel is almost completely impotent if its supernatural elements are taken out, for whatever reason. The resurrection of Jesus and our future resurrection cannot be metaphors only. One does not have to be an ignorant hermit to believe in the supernatural in the contemporary world. Scholarly evidence of contemporary supernatural healings abounds. A Christianity completely limited to the natural dimension of life is not biblical Christianity. It makes more sense to embrace both the natural and the supernatural dimensions of the Christian faith.

Let me present key biblical passages that give me assurance that we can boldly pray for the sick and expect healing.

1. God is a healer: "If you diligently heed the voice of the Lord your God and do what is right in His sight, give ear to His commandments and keep all His statutes, I will put none of the diseases on you which I have brought on the Egyptians. For I am the Lord who heals you" (Exod 15:26).

2. God's Word promises healing in response to anointing with oil and praying by faith: "And the prayer of faith shall save the sick, and the Lord shall raise him up; and if he have committed sins, they shall be forgiven him" (Jas 5:15 KJV).

   "They shall take up serpents; and if they drink any deadly thing, it shall not hurt them; they shall lay hands on the sick, and they shall recover" (Mark 16:18 KJV).

3. Jesus carried our sin and sickness to the cross of Calvary: "Surely he hath borne our griefs, and carried our sorrows: yet we did esteem him stricken, smitten of God, and afflicted" (Isa 53:4 KJV).

   ". . . that it might be fulfilled which was spoken by Esaias the prophet, saying, Himself took our infirmities, and bare our sicknesses" (Matt 8:17 KJV).

   "And immediately when Jesus perceived in his spirit that they so reasoned within themselves, he said unto them, Why reason ye these things in your hearts? Whether is it easier to say to the sick of the palsy, Thy sins be forgiven thee; or to say, Arise, and take up thy bed, and walk? But that ye may know that the Son of man hath power on earth to forgive sins, (he saith to the sick of the palsy,) I say unto thee, Arise, and take up thy bed, and go thy way into thine house" (Mark 2:8–11 KJV).

4. Jesus' mission included the work of healing: "The Spirit of the LORD is upon Me, because He has anointed Me to preach the gospel to the poor; He has sent Me to heal the brokenhearted, to proclaim liberty to the captives and recovery of sight to the blind, to set at liberty those who are oppressed" (Luke 4:18).

5. Jesus commanded, prepared, and empowered His disciples to heal the sick: "Then he called his twelve disciples together, and gave them power and authority over all devils, and to cure diseases. And he sent them to preach the kingdom of God, and to heal the sick" (Luke 9:1–2 KJV).

   "And He said to them, 'Go into all the world and preach the gospel to every creature. He who believes and is baptized will be saved; but he who does not believe will be condemned. And these signs will follow those who believe: In My name they will cast out demons; they will speak with new tongues; they will take up serpents; and if they drink anything deadly, it will by no means hurt them; they will lay hands on the sick, and they will recover'" (Mark 16:15–18).

6. Healing is a benefit of the kingdom of God. Healing can manifest where the gospel is preached: "And heal the sick that are therein, and say unto them, The kingdom of God is come nigh unto you" (Luke 10:9 KJV).

"And they went forth, and preached every where, the Lord working with them, and confirming the word with signs following. Amen" (Mark 16:20 KJV).

7. Healing is a gift of the Holy Spirit, who is still at work in the world. Howard Ervin called healing the Lord's "love gift" to His children: "Now there are diversities of gifts, but the same Spirit. . . . To another [is given] faith by the same Spirit; to another the gifts of healing by the same Spirit" (1 Cor 12:4, 9 KJV).[1]

8. The apostles' preaching connected healing and salvation, as Jesus had done earlier: "Be it known unto you all, and to all the people of Israel, that by the name of Jesus Christ of Nazareth, whom ye crucified, whom God raised from the dead, even by him doth this man stand here before you whole. . . . Neither is there salvation in any other: for there is none other name under heaven given among men, whereby we must be saved" (Acts 4:10, 12 KJV).

9. A Christian's body and spirit belong to God. We can glorify God with our bodies and spirits. The benefits of our salvation through faith in Jesus cannot be limited to the spirit alone: "What? know ye not that your body is the temple of the Holy Ghost which is in you, which ye have of God, and ye are not your own? For ye are bought with a price: therefore glorify God in your body, and in your spirit, which are God's" (1 Cor 6:19–20 KJV).

---

[1] Ervin, *Healing,* 14–29 (see chap. 2, n. 1).

10. Paul the apostle connected the sanctifying of the body with the sanctification of the soul and spirit: "And the very God of peace sanctify you wholly; and I pray God your whole spirit and soul and body be preserved blameless unto the coming of our Lord Jesus Christ" (1 Thess 5:23 KJV).

Church History

The ministry of healing continued throughout the history of the church. By the end of the New Testament, anointing with oil and praying for the sick was standard practice in the Christian church. The neglect of the healing ministry and its infiltration by ignorance and superstitions during the Middle Ages had understandable theological and historical reasons. The pride and arrogance of the Roman Empire, the theological deviations proposed by the brilliant minds of some of the church fathers, and gross ministry malpractice of the backslidden church contributed to the relegation of healing as a work of the marginalized or superstitious for a lengthy period. Thankfully, there have always been witnesses to the truth of God's healing power.

Brilliant theologians and great leaders, such as Augustine and Martin Luther, who once disavowed divine healing, later changed their minds based on further study and personal experiences. Although their initial position hindered this ministry of healing, their reversal is significant.

The Holiness Movement

The manner in which the doctrine of divine healing developed in the Holiness movement is significant. Not a host of heretics, but a compassionate group of ordinary Christians in Europe and the United States who were committed to a life of holiness rediscovered the truth of divine healing in the Word of God. People who took the words of Jesus seriously and desired to understand the full meaning of the atonement of Christ rediscovered the faith and practices of the early church. Moved by the suffering and pain in their world, many of these people embraced this truth and invested their lives in the ministry of healing. Men and women alike were involved in the development of this theology. Theologians and medical professionals were involved. Many received healing for themselves in this process, and they offered their services to others who needed healing. There were some radicals among them, denouncing doctors and medicine, but most of them were not hostile to physicians or medical treatment. For example, Dr. Cullis's faith home in Boston offered both prayer and medical care.

The Holiness people took theological issues such as the connection between healing and the atonement seriously. The question of whether divine healing is provided in the atonement has been discussed widely in both the Holiness and Pentecostal movements. There are several views on this matter that have been held by different groups and major personalities. The first view is that healing is provided in the atonement. The early Holiness movement, with its emphasis on complete sanctification, held this view. John Dowie and Kelso Carter initially held that healing is in the atonement, and therefore there is a guarantee of healing in all situations. Carter changed his position later and became less dogmatic in his ministry. Other leaders in the Holiness movement, such as A. B. Simpson, R. A. Torrey, A. J. Gordon, and others, believed that healing is provided in the atonement, but it is not an absolute guarantee. Historically, the group that believed that healing is not in the atonement included Horace Bushnell of Yale University and B. B. Warfield of Princeton. However, Bushnell held that healing represented God's sympathy, and Warfield considered healing a by-product of the atonement.

In the twentieth century, Oral Roberts, first as a Pentecostal and later as the father of the charismatic movement, believed that healing is in the atonement. His position was seen as an effort to balance the certainty or guarantee of healing through the atonement with God's sovereignty. John Wimber, leader of the Vineyard Fellowship, believed that although healing is not in the atonement, it is accomplished through the atonement. We can conclude that there is room to believe in praying for healing in all these views of the atonement.

Methods and Models of Healing

In a scholarly study of pastoral care, Charles R. Jaekle and William A. Clebsch have established from a careful historical survey that pastoral care had four different goals: healing, guiding, sustaining, and reconciling. They discovered that different periods in history demanded an emphasis on one of these. In my review, I discovered that healing appears to have remained a strong constant. Ronald Kydd, Ken Blue, and other scholars have categorized the various models of healing based on history, traditions, and theology. Following are eight different models that have been identified (among others).[2]

1. Confrontational: It is believed that early church fathers and pioneer divine healers of the Holiness movement practiced this model.

2. Intercessory: This is the model in which people expected the intervention of saints to accomplish healing.

3. Reliquial: This is where religious relics were used to bring about healing.

4. Incubation: This represents the healing homes established by Blumhardt, Trudell, Cullis, and others. Father Francis MacNutt's model of soaking prayer may be considered related to this model.

5. Revelational through word of knowledge: Pentecostal faith healers such as William M. Branham and Kathryn Kuhlman and leaders of the word of faith movement may be included in this category.

6. Soteriological: A. B. Simpson, Charles Price, and Oral Roberts may be placed in this model. Roberts called his method "healing evangelism."

7. Liturgical: Based on the apostle Paul's words in First Corinthians 11, this involved using the sacraments of the church to minister healing.

8. Pastoral healing: Based on James 5, the elders of the church minister healing. Pastoral care is considered a model of healing in this category. Oral Roberts's

---

[2] See R. A. N. Kydd, "Healing in the Christian Church," in S. M. Burgess, *NIDPCM,* 698–711.

emphasis on whole-person healing incorporated this method of healing. My model of pastoral care as ministry between miracles comes under this category.

The Pentecostals

The early Pentecostals adopted the teaching of divine healing as a core doctrine, and I had the opportunity to observe it as theology and practice. The full gospel always included healing. The Pentecostal gospel was a foursquare gospel: Jesus saves; Jesus heals; Jesus baptizes with the Holy Spirit; Jesus is coming again. I have seen both Pentecostals and charismatics minister healing through the prayer of faith in several nations. My family members and I have experienced the power of faith and prayer. I have prayed for thousands of people as a chaplain at a place where prayer and medicine were merged. I heard many testimonies of healing there. My family has experienced healing through prayer and medicine. As I mentioned earlier, we have family members who prayed for the sick and demonstrably saw many healings. I have received testimonies of healing from people I prayed for in different places.

We have closely examined the legacies and theologies of two world-renowned practitioners of healing ministry: healing evangelist Oral Roberts from the West and Pastor David Yonggi Cho from the East. Both ministers demonstrated a charismatic approach to prayer and healing. Oral Roberts moved through three demonstrable stages of development in his theology of healing: from Pentecostal "divine healing" to charismatic "signs and wonders" to Spirit-empowered "whole person healing."[3] The writings of David Yonggi Cho, founding pastor of the largest local congregation in the world, reveal a well-read person. It is not reasonable to dismiss their healing ministries or relegate the impact and lasting outcomes of their lives to a lack of theological sophistication or some clever capacity to inflict mass manipulation. Even those who may have disagreements with certain aspects of their theologies must acknowledge that their lives and ministries affirmed the Bible and enhanced faith in a healing God.

Pentecostals and charismatics have their share of charlatans, imitators, manipulators, and fake healers, but they are a small minority and are regularly exposed. I know hundreds of sincere pastors and believers, on the other hand, who gain nothing tangible from praying for the sick except the joy of seeing someone's suffering end, when it happens. They do not deny suffering. They do not receive payments. They do not want to be celebrities. They believe in healing through prayer but do not guarantee healing always and in every situation because they live by faith humbly between biblical certainty of healing and God's sovereignty.

Radicals and Cessationists

Both the Holiness movement and the Pentecostal/charismatic movement have had their share of radicals who reject doctors and hospitals. They believe that reaching out for medical care is an expression of lack of faith. However, we have seen from our review of the history of hospitals that medical

---

[3] Mathew, "Oral Roberts' Theology of Healing" (see chap. 8, n. 1).

and nursing care are an outgrowth of the healing legacy of Jesus. Jesus' radical teaching about one's neighbor and His command to care for the needy and to heal the sick resulted in the formation of the first real hospital in the world. The early Christians were identified by their compassion and care for the poor and needy and were ridiculed by some and admired by others for it. Although the modern medical establishment, especially in America, has become an impersonal industrial complex, physicians, nurses, and other medical professionals are not the enemies of God or the good news of Jesus Christ. As they use their knowledge and skills to enhance the healing capacity in the human body created by God, they can be considered ministers of natural healing, especially those who are committed to a whole-person approach to medicine, just as Christian ministers, medical professionals, and all followers of Jesus who pray for the sick by faith can be seen as ministers of both natural and supernatural healing.

The cessationists have not convinced me that God has put Himself in a first-century time capsule. I do not believe that a Christianity void of all supernatural dimensions is Christianity at all. It is something other than biblical Christianity. I do not wish to throw out a biblical truth because some have chosen to abuse it. I recognize that all good currency is counterfeited. That should not cause one to stop using the good currency. Many cessationists choose to interpret passages such as 1 Peter 2:24—"[Christ] Himself bore our sins in His own body on the tree, that we, having died to sins, might live for righteousness—by whose stripes you were healed"—as future benefits of believers, not having any immediate application.

I hope cessationists will reconsider their rigid position in this postmodern age.

I do not believe that only people without a good theology of suffering can pray for the sick by faith and expect healing. An adequate theology of suffering and the doctrine of divine healing are not mutually exclusive. I also believe that Pentecostal overreaction to extreme-prosperity teachers is unwise. Over-stretching of a truth by some should not cause abandonment of the real truth by others.

The church has confessed the healing power of Jesus' name for two thousand years. The Scriptures, the apostolic fathers, and the entire history of the church bear witness to God's power and His willingness to heal. We should not abandon this heritage completely. Divine healing is a sound doctrine like any orthodox Christian doctrine, especially when God's sovereignty is part of the doctrine and there is room made for both medicine and prayer, both natural and supernatural healing.

Applying the Quadrilateral and Ervin's Grid

The doctrine of divine healing passes the test of the Methodist quadrilateral, which is a grid to look through—Scripture, tradition, reason, and experience—to validate a belief. I am convinced that the Scriptures support the doctrine of divine healing. Church history confirms the Christian tradition of healing. Modern science and whole-person medicine convince us that the prayer of faith can promote healing and health. And there is an abundance of experience spanning two thousand years affirming the possibility of healing through faith and prayer.

I applied another method of validation to the teaching of divine healing. I learned this method from my revered professor and later honored colleague at Oral Roberts University, Howard M. Ervin. He advised me to ask the following five questions regarding a questionable teaching before affirming its truthfulness:

1. Does it have biblical witness? (Does the Bible support healing through prayer?)
2. Does it have historical witness? (Has healing through prayer manifested in the history of the church?)
3. Does it have existential witness? (Is healing taking place through prayer in the world currently?)
4. Does it have personal witness? (Have you experienced healing through prayer personally?)
5. Does it have spiritual witness? (Does the Holy Spirit bear witness with your spirit that God heals in response to the prayer of faith offered in the name of Jesus?)

My answer to all of Ervin's questions is a resounding "YES!"

Conclusion

We began this study by looking at health and healing in the Hebrew Bible. We then examined healing and wholeness in the New Testament, particularly in the life and ministry of Jesus and His disciples. We traced the history of healing ministry from the first century through the post-Reformation period and focused on the development and clarification of the doctrine of divine healing within the intercontinental Holiness movement. We then examined its adoption and practice within the Pentecostal/charismatic (Spirit-empowered) movement.

We reviewed the history of hospitals and the medical profession and discovered that medical care of the sick is a legacy of Jesus. The unique contributions of the whole-person model of medical care are even more so. We have studied two well-known twentieth-century teachers and practitioners of the healing ministry in terms of the theologies undergirding their practices. We examined the unique lessons about natural and divine healing learned from the founding of the former City of Faith Hospital to merge medicine and prayer on the campus of Oral Roberts University. We took the concerns raised by the cessationists and other skeptics seriously and addressed them. I am fully convinced at this point that God heals the sick naturally and supernaturally. He responds to the prayer of faith for healing and wholeness offered in the name of Jesus. I believe that all pastors, physicians, and Christians should pray for the sick by faith, expecting healing.

***

Thank you for accompanying me on this journey of inquiry. I hope you enjoyed the learning and discovery as much as I did and that you also have concluded that God is a good God and that He heals. I hope you have developed an appreciation for both whole-person medicine and the power of the prayer of faith and that you will trust God to answer your prayers for healing—for yourself and others—in both natural and supernatural ways. Certainly, God is a good God. He is not limited by the natural. As the past, present, and future are all known to our God at the same time, so also are the natural and the supernatural dimensions in His purview. Be encouraged, dear reader, to pray for the sick, and be emboldened to expect healing.

BIBLIOGRAPHY

Burgess, Stanley M., ed. *The New International Dictionary of Pentecostal and Charismatic Movements*. Rev. and expanded ed. Grand Rapids: Zondervan, 2002.

Bonhoeffer, Dietrich. *Creation and Fall*. New York: Macmillan, 1959; reprint ed., n. d.

Buttrick, George A. *God, Pain, and Evil*. Nashville: Abingdon, 1966.

Calvin, John. *Institutes of the Christian Religion*. Louisville: Westminster John Knox Press, 1960.

Chappell, Paul Gale. *Great Things He Hath Done: Origins of the Divine Healing Movement in America*. Unpublished course reader, ORU College of Theology and Ministry. Based on Chappell, Paul Gale. "The Divine Healing Movement in America." PhD thesis, Drew University, 1983.

_____. "Origins of the Divine Healing Movement in America." *Spiritus: ORU Journal of Theology* 1, no. 1, article 3 (1985).

Cho, David Yonggi. *Born to Be Blessed*. Seoul: Seoul Logos, 1993.

_____. *Church Growth, Do You Really Want It?* (1995). Quoted in Myung Soo Park, "David Yonggi Cho and International Pentecostal/Charismatic Movements," *2002 Young San International Theological Symposium*. Korea: Hansei University, 2002.

_____. *The Fourth Dimension.* 3rd ed. Seoul: Seoul Logos, 1979.

_____. *The Fourth Dimension.* Vol. 2. South Plainfield, NJ: Bridge, 1979, 1983.

_____. *How Can I Be Healed?* Seoul: Seoul Logos, 1999.

_____. *Salvation, Health, and Prosperity: Our Threefold Blessings in Christ.* Altamonte Springs, FL: Creation House Strang Communications, 1987.

_____. *Use Your Faith Energy.* Seoul: Seoul Logos, 2004.

Clebsch, W. A., and C. R. Jaekle. *Pastoral Care in Historical Perspective.* Englewood Cliffs, NJ: Prentice Hall, 1964.

Dayton, Donald. *Theological Roots of Pentecostalism.* Grand Rapids: Baker Academic, 1987.

Dubovsky, H. "The Jewish Contribution to Medicine. Part I. Biblical and Talmudic Times to the End of the 18th Century." *South African Medical Journal,* July 1, 1989.

Elwell, Walter A. *Evangelical Dictionary of Theology.* 2nd ed. Grand Rapids: Baker Academic, 2001.

Ervin, Howard M. *Healing: Sign of the Kingdom.* Peabody, MA: Hendrickson, 2002.

Ferngren, Gary B. *Medicine and Health Care in Early Christianity.* Baltimore: Johns Hopkins University, 2009.

Floriani, Peter J. *An Introduction to the History of the Hospital.* N.p.: independently published, 2018.

Gerstenberger, E. S., and W. Schrage. *Suffering.* Translated by John E. Steely. Nashville: Abingdon, 1980.

Harrell, David E., Jr. *All Things Are Possible: The Healing and Charismatic Revivals in America.* Bloomington: Indiana University Press, 1975.

Hyatt, Eddie L. *2000 Years of Charismatic Christianity.* Lake Mary, FL: Charisma House, 2002.

Irish, Kerry E. "The Great Awakening and the Coming of the American Revolution" (2022). *Faculty Publications— Department of History and Politics.* https://digitalcommons. georgefox.edu/hist_fac/100.

Jones, E. Stanley. *Christ and Human Suffering.* New York: Abingdon, 1933.

Keener, Craig S. *Miracles Today: The Supernatural Work of God in the Modern World.* Grand Rapids: Baker Academic, 2021.

Kelsey, Morton. *Healing and Christianity.* New York: HarperCollins, 1976.

Kendall, R. T. *Holy Fire: A Balanced, Biblical Look at the Work of the Holy Spirit in Our Lives.* Lake Mary: FL: Charisma House, 2014.

Kydd, Ronald A. D. *Healing through the Centuries.* Carol Stream, IL: Tyndale House, 1998.

Lee, Younghoon. "Oral Roberts and David Yonggi Cho: A Life-Long Relationship in Theology and Ministry." *Spiritus: ORU Journal of Theology* 4, no. 1, article 4 (2019).

Lewis, C. S. *The Problem of Pain.* New York: Macmillan, 1962.

Ma, Wonsuk, ed. *David Yonggi Cho: A Close Look at His Theology and Ministry.* Baguio, Philippines: APTS Press, 2004.

MacArthur, John. *Strange Fire: The Danger of Offending the Holy Spirit with Counterfeit Worship.* Nashville: Nelson Books, 2013.

Mathew, Saju. *Kerala Penthekosthu Charithram*: *The History of Pentecost in Kerala.* 2nd Malayalam ed. Kottayam, Kerala, India: Goodnews Books, 2007.

Mathew, Thomson K. *Ministry Between Miracles: A Biblical Model of Spirit-led Pastoral Care.* Kottayam, Kerala, India: Goodnews Books, 2020.

_____. "Oral Roberts and David Yonggi Cho: A Comparative Evaluation of Their Theologies of Healing."

Dr. Yonggi Cho's Ministry & Theology. Vol. 1. Gunpo, Korea: Hansei University Logos, 2008.

_____. "Oral Roberts' Theology of Healing: A Journey from Pentecostal 'Divine Healing' to Charismatic 'Signs and Wonders' to Spirit-Empowered 'Whole Person Healing'." *Spiritus: ORU Journal of Theology* 3, no. 2, article 13 (2018).

Muthalali, Jacob. *Heal the Sick in the Name of Jesus.* N.p.: Author, 2006.

Nouwen, Henri J. M. *The Living Reminder: Service and Prayer in Memory of Jesus.* New York: HarperCollins, 1977.

Park, Myung Soo. "David Yonggi Cho and International Pentecostal/Charismatic Movements." *2002 Young San International Theological Symposium.* Korea: Hansei University, 2002.

Roberts, Oral. *Better Health and Miracle Living.* Tulsa, OK: Oral Roberts Evangelistic Association, 1976.

_____. *Expect a Miracle: My Life and Ministry.* Nashville: Thomas Nelson, 1995.

_____. *If You Need Healing, Do These Things.* Tulsa, OK: Oral Roberts Ministries, 2002.

_____. *Miracles of Healing for You Today.* Tulsa, OK: Oral Roberts Ministries, 1982.

_____. *3 Most Important Steps to Your Better Health and Miracle Living.* Tulsa, OK: Oral Roberts Evangelistic Association, 1976.

_____. *Holy Bible with Personal Commentary by Oral Roberts.* Tulsa, OK: Oral Roberts Evangelistic Association, 1981.

Saji, B. *Oru Pravachakante Preshitha Yathra: A Prophet's Missionary Journey.* Kayamkulam, Kerala, India: Mizpah, 2003.

Walsh, James J. *The Catholic Church and Healing.* New York: MacMillan, 1928.

White, Ellen. *Good Health* (1880–1889), https://egwwritings.
org/book/b440.

Wood, George P., ed. *Influence: The Shape of Leadership.*
Springfield, MO: General Council of the Assemblies of
God, 2022.

Yancey, Philip. *Where Is God When It Hurts?* Grand Rapids:
Zondervan, 1977.

Youmans, Roger L. *Healing Team Concepts Manual.* Unpublished
class reader, ORU School of Medicine, 1989.

ALSO BY THOMSON K. MATHEW

Ministry Between Miracles

A Seminary Dean's Experiment with Servant Leadership

Spiritual Identity and Spirit-Empowered Life

Spiritual Identity and Spirit-Empowered Life Leader's Guide

Spirit-led Ministry in the Twenty-First Century

What Will Your Tombstone Say?

Ministry Research Simplified

51644173R00161